THE PRIMARY HEAD'S SURVIVAL GUIDE

Heinemann Educational
Halley Court, Jordan Hill, Oxford OX2 8EJ
a division of Reed Educational and Professional Publishing Ltd

OXFORD FLORENCE PRAGUE MADRID ATHENS
MELBOURNE AUCKLAND KUALA LUMPUR SINGAPORE TOKYO
IBADAN NAIROBI KAMPALA JOHANNESBURG GABORONE
PORTSMOUTH NH (USA) CHICAGO MEXICO CITY SAO PAULO

© Mary St-Amour and Ian Stevens
First published 1996

00 99 98 97 96
10 9 8 7 6 5 4 3 2 1

ISBN 0 435 80919 9

Typeset by Books Unlimited (Nottm)
Printed in England by Clays Ltd, St Ives plc

THE PRIMARY HEAD'S SURVIVAL GUIDE

MARY ST-AMOUR
AND
IAN STEVENS

Heinemann

About the authors:

Mary St-Amour and Ian Stevens are headteachers in Milton Keynes, Buckinghamshire, with In-service Masters' Degrees in Education from the Open University and Leicester University. Committed as they are to excellence in primary education, they are both involved in Initial Teacher Education and In-service Teacher Training, and also in training Governors.

Ian has two children and Mary has four. This gives them a further insight into primary, secondary and higher education from the parent's point of view (and likewise the child's).

DEDICATION

To all the children, governors, parents and colleagues with whom we have worked, are working, and will work in the future. May we together draw nearer our common goal of excellent education for all.

Staff.
Staff Policy (Draft)

3 abs, in 3 months. - cause concern
6 abs in 6 months - Staff to examine

- 7 days self certification
- Dr's note
- peer group pressure...

ABSENCES

The most difficult absences to deal with amongst children and staff are those which you suspect are not genuine. They need to be investigated thoroughly. For children, frequent unexplained absences will impair learning and social development and possibly lead to reduced life chances. With staff, the results can generate a climate of mistrust and resentment, as well as making extra work for colleagues.

With children, clear procedures for checking registers and reporting suspect absences are essential. These should be spelt out in your prospectus. Staff must know when to alert you to a non-attender. Parents need to know at what point they should contact the school when their child is away – and whether by phone or letter.

The Education Welfare Officer may also need to be involved. It is up to you to decide when that is appropriate. For frequent non-attenders or truants, you need to investigate fully. A child may be under pressure to stay away from school to help run the home, or to conceal physical, or sexual abuse. (*See* TRUANCY.)

With staff, self-certification makes it difficult to nail the habitual absentee. You, your colleagues and the children have a right to expect members of staff to deliver the goods. And you have the right to know *why* a member of staff is away. Without any reason given and no excuse for not giving one, you may assume that the reason is not illness. You may then guide your governors, and the LEA if appropriate, on whether leave of absence should be approved or not; paid or unpaid.

Above all, where you have suspicions, it is essential to document staff absences over a reasonable period of time. Note any patterns which emerge. Discuss the situation with the staff member and explain your concerns. Offer help and support. Try to find out causes. If they originate at school, do something about them. Ask for medical certificates and a full medical with the LEA doctor if you have concerns about mental or physical fitness. Record everything you do. But be quite clear: a staff member who is absent continually for no substantial reason must either find a solution or find a new career! Children and their learning are too important.

ACCIDENTS

Accidents will happen in school. Most result in scraped knees or bruises. But every accident needs investigation. Accidents caused by faulty equipment or lack of supervision are potentially serious and could lead to litigation, or worse. How they are dealt with comes within your responsibility for day-to-day management. Your Governing Body may have in place routines specifically for dealing with accidents and emergencies, which are part of their Health and Safety Policy: you should follow these to the letter. If it does not, you need to agree with your whole staff the action to be taken when an accident occurs. An accident form or checklist is useful. This makes sure that everyone follows the procedures calmly and nothing is overlooked. It also covers you and the governing body if an accident occurs while you are off-site.

The following points may be useful:

- The over-riding duty is to secure prompt medical attention for the injured person (*See* FIRST AID).

- An accident book should be kept in which to record *all* accidents, minor as well as serious. A record should be kept stating the nature of the accident, *time, date, nature, treatment* and *initials/signature* of the person administering treatment.

- Encourage your staff to use water compresses/ice/bandages/ tender loving care, etc., as opposed to creams or plasters. The latter treatments may well make you liable to repercussions in a Court if something goes wrong.

- If deemed appropriate, parents should be contacted at the earliest opportunity. You are responsible for decisions taken in the child's interest until parents/guardians arrive.

- You must also exercise the same quality of care and procedure for adults.

- Make sure everyone knows who is taking charge in all accident cases. Assign individuals to do certain tasks (as appropriate), e.g. ringing for ambulances, making an area safe, supervision of children, contacting parents or partners.

- Gather as much detailed information as you can from those who witnessed those accidents which you deem necessary to follow up. Make sure procedures have been followed. Use the information to take immediate remedial action to eliminate further risks to others.

● Complete Health and Safety forms if the accident involves fractures or more serious injury. Send these forms at once to the relevant bodies.

We urge you to be pro-active in encouraging all staff to follow these guidelines. Never under-estimate any accident: an unrecorded accident may well turn out to be serious. An injured child or adult may subsequently generate symptoms that could prove fatal. You will sleep at night if you know the correct procedures have been followed. You have done the best you can. And have the evidence to prove it. *(See also DISASTERS.)*

ACCOUNTABILITY
What is accountability?
- audit
- responsibility
- explanation
- action
- reasons
- reckoning
- maintenance
- liability

As head:
- To whom are you accountable?
- Why should you be accountable?
- How are you accountable?
- What has made you accountable?

You are accountable to: children, parents, governors, LEA, DFE, the public, all staff, Ofsted. You are accountable to those you serve, your clients! You are accountable because your clients are entitled to access a broad, balanced and differentiated curriculum. The children in your care deserve the very best. You are accountable for what you produce.

This will be judged by the following:
- the number of children who attend your school
- SATS results
- league tables
- the size of your budget
- sports achievement

- academic standards
- behavioural aspirations
- the type of pupil you attract.

All this provided the climate for the emergence of the Education Reform Act (1988). Few would dispute that this could be described as the most important piece of educational legislation since 1944!

As Joan Sallis queried (1988) "Are you subject to professional accountability or organised interference?"

Whatever the answer, as head you need to be conscious of your accounting role. In order to be constantly aware, put into place systems that deal daily with accountability. Be confident in your responses and remain in control!

ADVERTISEMENTS

Advertising for a member of staff is the second step in a costly and time-consuming process. The first is to be certain that you actually need someone! Look carefully at your current staffing. Could you re-allocate responsibilities to bring fresh challenge and vitality to jaded job allocations? Do you have a part-time teacher desperate to work full-time? Could you increase the size of your classes and use the money saved to buy computers or other much-needed equipment?

Governors must be involved throughout the whole process of recruitment. Agree on precise job and person specifications at the outset. Work back from the start of the contract. Choose the best time to advertise. Adverts which appear in the *Times Educational Supplement* in the last week of the Autumn term can't compete with Christmas planning. Choose where you will place the advertisement. For senior posts, national advertising will get you into most schools in the country. But it is expensive, especially if you have to pay travel and overnight expenses. So negotiate a price before you place it and try for a good deal on logo, length and positioning. Other posts, advertised in the "free" or local papers prompt a more immediate response. Most LEAs have an internal jobs circular. This is free advertising and is essential reading for local teachers looking for a new job.

Make sure that the advertisement contains the essential

information. Describe your school, its size and position, with a line or two about your ethos and practice. Is the post permanent or temporary and are you flexible over the starting date? What are the key responsibilities? What are the arrangements for visits and are you available to discuss the post over the phone? What is the salary and is this negotiable? When are the interviews to be held? Is application to be by letter or by form and when is the closing date?

Other posts for cleaners, meals supervisors and office staff should follow the same pattern. Don't forget that the simplest advertising is often the best. That card in the newsagent's window or simple word-of-mouth may bring a posse of likely candidates to your door the very next day!

ADVISERS AND INSPECTORS
Most LEAs have advisers or inspectors who look after clusters or groups of schools. The problems for many are that the demands of Ofsted inspecting and delivering In-Service training reduce the amount of time for general support of schools.

The role of the primary head can be a lonely one: an experienced adviser, with a background in primary education, can provide tremendous support in times of need.

The problems that arise usually do so from a lack of clarity about the role of the adviser. Many advisers live in a twilit world of conflicting demands: the "Framework for Inspection" in one hand and a copy of Kyriacrou's "Essential Teaching Skills" in the other. Plan out with your adviser or inspector a programme for the whole year. Agree on the number of visits and the work that needs to be done. Inset, pre-Ofsted, observation, assessment, governor training should all be within the range of the services offered by the LEA in support of sc hools.

Her Majesty's Inspectors are a rare species and you are unlikely to get a visit, unless they are heading Ofsted teams.

AGE OF TRANSFER
The ages at which children enter formal education and transfer from phase to phase vary within the United Kingdom.

Primary education can be from:
- 4-plus to 12
- 4-plus to 8
- 5 to 7
- 5 to 11.

Most heads, parents and governors would agree that children are ready to start formal schooling after their fourth birthday. A structured learning environment in nursery, leading to a rich early-years curriculum, gives children a flying start.

Transition from infant and first schools can be at seven, eight or nine.

Transfer to secondary education can be at eleven, twelve or thirteen, depending upon the authority in which you work. The age at which children ideally transfer to secondary education is a matter of debate. Those who favour middle schools, recognise that for many children greater maturity on transfer at age 12 or 13, allows them to cope more easily with the change.

The National Curriculum, with its Key Stages based upon the traditional transfers at 7 and 11, coupled with reductions in primary school roll, has prompted some LEAs to re-consider ages of transfer.

But, ages of transfer matter little. The fundamental issue is whether children are receiving a curriculum which is matched to both their needs and entitlement.

Re-visit, re-evaluate and re-establish your primary philosophy!

ANTS, WASPS AND BEES
Airborne and ambulant ants are a seasonal curse. The Bible has the best advice:
"Go to the ant, thou sluggard; consider her ways and be wise." (*Proverbs vi.*)

So organise a crash course in entomology for your caretaker. Several minutes in a corridor with your science specialist should do the trick. Armed with this basic knowledge and some cans of powder, your caretaker will soon relish the annual battle of wits and prevent the creatures from eating the childrens' lunches.

Wasps and bees can cause the occasional panic. So the following precautions will be helpful:

- Make sure that you have a supply of anti-histamine spray.
- Find out if any of your children, or adults, is likely to suffer from extreme reaction to stings.
- Get your caretaker to check regularly for nests.
- Always call parents and partners if a child or adult is stung.
- Always remember that reactions to stings, for some people, may be sudden and life-threatening: so always call an ambulance if you are concerned.

Try to make sure that anti-ant attacks and wasp nest removals are carried out before, or after, the school day. And definitely avoid those times when Buddhist festivals are the Assembly theme for that week.

APPRAISAL

Few would argue that teachers and heads have mixed feelings about the purposes of appraisal. What are the real purposes and how can they be achieved? The main ones, historically speaking, can be seen to fall into at least five categories:

- developing a clarity of vision, direction and purpose in the organisation
- maintaining and building on that vision, direction and purpose
- evaluation of the staff resources of the organisation
- developing and improving the skills and career prospects of individual members of staff
- capitalising on individual and organisational strengths for the mutual benefit of all contributors, including the pupils.

Like so many other educational developments, appraisal was imposed upon the profession. In this case it was through the Education (School Teacher Appraisal) Regulations 1991.

Remember however, that the general purpose of appraisal is one of professional development. Most models include self-appraisal with a vehicle for observation and dialogue, involving peers and usually the head. Developmental targets form the outcomes, which will, hopefully, positively influence Inset provision and whole-school development.

Where are the obstacles?
- time
- management of the process
- the development of unrealistic expectations
- budgetary implications
- winning mutual respect of appraiser/appraisee
- gaining commitment to appraisal
- hidden agendas.

Many feel that appraisal is only a precursor to payment by results! By taking part in the process, as head, are you paving the way for this to become reality? Ask yourself, however, if you can afford not to! And remember, at what other time in your life will you have the opportunity of someone listening solely to you, for a prescribed amount of time? How often are people willing to listen to your problems? Your appraisers have to, as part of the appraisal process. So why not, as always, proceed with caution, and make the most of it!

ASSEMBLIES

Coming together for Assembly gives children the sense of being part of the community, which is a central part of school life. For the headteacher, who leads the community, it is a special opportunity to guide and shape the values which good primary education promotes. Children come to see themselves as part of a community which values them and to which they can contribute. They also learn to develop a sense of responsibility for others.

But assembling children is not enough. The Education Reform Act requires a daily act of collective worship, which should be "wholly or mainly of a broadly Christian character". In county schools the responsibility for this rests with you.

The use of the word "collective" as opposed to "corporate" is deliberate. The 1944 Act recognised that not all children would be Christian and would bring different beliefs to school. Some children will come from agnostic and atheist backgrounds, for whom the notion of worship is unacceptable.

The commonsense approach is to see Assembly as a special time of togetherness which is different from the rest of the day. This time may can be used to explore values and ideas through stories, drama, music and quiet reflection. Using stories and ideas from other cultures and religions does not deprive an act of worship of its Christian character, but enhances it.

ASSERTIVENESS

To put oneself forward in an authoritative manner while being positive and always in control, is to provide assertive leadership in action. In any situation involving other people, we usually have a range of behaviour options open to us; it is therefore useful to:

- consider the situation
- choose the response
- evaluate the desired consequence.

Depending upon the situation, we can be aggressive, passive or assertive.

As an aggressive head you express your opinions and feelings so forcibly that the other person feels punished, put down or threatened. As a passive head you hope that you will get what you want in leaving it to chance. As an assertive head you tell someone directly what you want in such a way that the other person is not put down and is respected. In acting assertively, the three main dimensions expressed tend to be:

- the expression of positive feelings
- expressing negative feelings constructively
- standing up for one's rights without violating the rights of others.

Being assertive is an important part of taking responsibility for oneself, in aiding self-esteem, reducing stress and in improving relationships with others.

What is important in true assertiveness?

Considering the importance of the issue and remembering that assertiveness takes energy and time and therefore may not be always worth it. Timing is crucial:

Never:
- respond assertively at the height of emotional feelings
- respond assertively when the other person is busy or pre-occupied.

Always:
- know what you want
- pick your time and place
- be clear and specific
- display confident bodily language
- be prepared to negotiate and compromise
- use concise and simple language
- be confident and assured
- criticise constructively
- be honest.

Don't hide behind your role; be yourself! Remember, assertiveness equals security and success, but never complacency.

ASSESSMENT

To ensure quality is encouraged and sustained in all areas of school life, your teachers are continually assessing skills, understanding and attitudes, as well as attainment within the post-Dearing National Curriculum. As head, you must maintain a climate in which all your pupils fulfil their potential. You must ensure that your staff measure, record and can account for individual achievement.

Problems are likely to arise if, as a staff:
- you do not share a common understanding of the functions of assessment
- you have not planned out a yearly assessment programme
- you have not reflected on effective teaching and learning strategies and attendant assessment processes
- you have not considered and developed a whole-school procedure of reporting pupil progress to parents

- you have not got a system in place to record progress and assessment.

It is worth evaluating with your staff what form **informal** and **formal** assessment are to take, and when they are to take place within your school.

Assessment should be a positive, informative and constructive process for pupils and staff. This can only be successfully achieved if the assessment process is planned for within the timetable.

BASICS

"Back to the basics". Just how many times have you heard that term? It is worth considering just what the basics are.

The basics in scholastic terms are the fundamentals: the simple elements of literacy and numeracy skills that underpin all learning for your pupils. They are an undefined, but presumed essential, standard in society.

You will achieve a basic standard for most children if:
- you have a well-structured whole-school approach to the curriculum
- there's a commonality in teaching and learning strategies
- the teaching of literacy and numeracy skills is structured and inherent in all learning experiences
- quality time is given to all pupils
- support systems are well planned
- a broad, balanced and differentiated curriculum is delivered
- long, medium and short-term planning is balanced and thorough
- informal and formal assessment processes are intrinsic in your learning programme
- children are happy, secure, stimulated, challenged and valued
- aims and objectives are regularly clarified
- targeting processes are put into place as appropriate
- a parental partnership is nurtured.

If you aspire to high but achievable standards in all areas, most children will exceed your expectations. Remember that children are individuals and will therefore develop at different rates. This is catered for in your school's curriculum-planning. Consider investing in good quality books and materials to stimulate interest. Tatty, uninteresting books will not encourage children to read or want to find out more. Research the market. Consider the exploitation of information technology in promoting the basic skills. Do not only rely on traditional methodology.

In your attempt to provide the best for your pupils: nurture life-long readers and problem-solvers. Give them *more* than the basics.

BETRAYAL
You will feel betrayed on many occasions in your role as head. Any form of betrayal is disappointing, but it can be an unfortunate reality. You must not dwell on any disloyalty. You will gradually learn to come to terms with deception.

Betrayal is experienced in many forms and to varying degrees. Basically betrayal is about disclosing a confidence, breaking a promise, undermining, double-crossing or disloyalty.

How will betrayal be manifest?
- in a governor disclosing a Governing Body confidence
- a member/s of staff undermining your philosophy and ethos
- mis-information being deliberately spread in an attempt to damage your sense of honour
- parents attempting to undermine your management of the school through treacherous methods
- any conspiracy
- pupils who "break all the rules".

Remember that not all acts of betrayal are intentional. Whether they are deliberate or not, you will be wise to keep a sense of perspective. They will be times when you *will* need to respond, to retaliate: but be measured in any reciprocation. You will be compensated if you *are* measured, objective, calm and in control. Retribution will not be experienced if you seek vengeance while emotional, hurt or angry. You will regain ground through planned, composed and assertive actions.

No matter how difficult your role is, never be tempted to indulge in beguiling methodology yourself!

Integrity is *EVERYTHING* in headship.

BICYCLES

You have a shared interest with parents in how children make their journeys to and from school. If children misbehave on the bus or shoplift between home and school, society expects you to demonstrate your concern and usually do something about it. The decision to allow children to cycle to school should not be taken lightly by parents or you. Before doing so, consider the following:

- Is it safe and practical to encourage your children to ride to school, bearing in mind the location of your school and the density of traffic?
- What do your governors think?
- All the year round, or just in the summer?
- Whom will you allow to ride? Those who have reached a certain age and/or passed a cycling awareness course?
- Will you insist on helmets being worn – and how do you enforce this?
- Who is responsible for the children's safety, to and from school?
- Which entrances will the children use? How can you keep cyclists apart from staff cars and delivery vehicles?
- Where will the children keep their bikes? Do you have proper secure cycle parking facilities?
- Are there implications for additional school insurance?

It may not be practicable – and so you will probably breathe a sigh of relief. But don't forget that most children ride a bike at some time. If you provide a form of road safety training, you will be helping them and others. Your local Road Safety Co-ordinator should be keen to start cycling awareness courses at your school, although you'll probably need to help by twisting the arms of parents to be volunteer tutors!

Staff, including heads!

Some of your staff may be cyclists. You might even pedal to school yourself! It may well be your way of keeping fit, your attempt to give your body tone, your blood circulation system cleared-out, and your mind unburdened.

In inner-cities and towns, a bike is a faster means of transport than a train, bus or car. If staff do cycle to school, then you need to provide secure accommodation for their bicycles. If you decide to cycle, then you need to consider how you cope with dress suitable for cycling and to conduct your role as head. Can you really spend your day in a tracksuit and trainers? If not, how do you carry your suits to school and where do you change? How do you get to meetings? If time allows, by bike, if not, you could try the occasional taxi.

Cycling could be the ultimate way to unwind. No way can you carry your overloaded briefcase on your bicycle and so you have to leave unfinished work at school. Who knows, cycling could stop you from becoming a workaholic!

BOILERS

Do not underestimate the importance of your school boiler. The efficient running of your boiler could be crucial to the maintenance of your site and the successful management of your finances. The unexpected cost of repairing your boiler could totally unbalance your annual financial plan.

Ensure that your caretaker understands the machinations of your boiler. Check that they are using the heating system to advantage. Visit your boiler-room regularly to see how well it is being kept. Question whether or not the boiler and room is being kept clean and tidy. Consider whether or not it should be used as a storage area.

Things to do:
- have regular meetings with your caretaker, discuss their job description and clarify your expectations in relation to care of the heating system; provide training for your caretaker as necessary
- monitor the maintenance of your heating system
- involve your governors
- be realistic in assigning funds
- liaise with contractors as appropriate.

It is in your interest to make yourself aware of how your boiler system works. Discourage lots of people from using the system. It will be best managed if it is cared for by as few as possible.

Your boiler is essential to the day-to-day workings of your school. Ensure that it is given the tender loving care it deserves.

The boiler might well benefit if it is allowed to be your caretaker's baby!

BOUNDARIES

The Education Reform Act (1988) highlights the importance of managing our organisational boundaries. In providing effective education, we must grow as institutions, in order to survive! The ERA raises a multitude of questions about parents' motives for choosing a school.

- How sensitive are parents and governors to the differences between schools?
- Who will they listen to?
- Where will they get their information from?
- How will their perceptions be formed?
- To what extent are individual decisions affected by informal networks and group-pressure?

How much influence can you exercise as head?

... and all things being equal, is it worth any amount of effort?

... at the end of the day, how important is it for schools to adapt to changing external conditions?

What do you need to do to survive?

Parents and governors are now more actively involved in schools than ever before, and any educational practitioner who fails to recognise this, does so at their own peril!

Make sure that your Governing Body works within its legal boundaries and has terms of reference for committees and working groups. Agree on collective responsibility, confidentiality and the status of minutes and reports.

"Senior officials must strike a balance between giving up total control of the group, and holding too tightly to the reins.

Delegation, in its optimal sense, means initially setting the parameters, then staying involved..."

(*What's Worth Fighting for in Headship*, Michael Fullan, 1992.)

BUILDINGS

Problems with buildings are almost always attributed to either basic design or lack of money, or to both! Too often, buildings are the scapegoats for poor achievement, low staff morale, or unacceptable behaviour among the children.

But the most dilapidated or antiquated schools are sometimes centres of excellence, vibrant with the excitement of children learning. As a head, you have to exercise your creative skill in constructing an environment where quality teaching and learning can take place. Every building has its advantages. The most austere Victorian building will have more room than its modern successors. It will certainly be cooler in summer, have more wall space for display and fittings to defy the most determined vandal. Later buildings, however, are more likely to suit modern teaching styles, be more attractive visually and encourage a sense of identity with the local community.

Whatever the age or state of the building you take over, start by addressing the needs of the children. It should be secure, healthy and safe. Only then can you develop an environment in which the curriculum can be delivered, and where all those who are engaged in it will feel valued and challenged to do their best. *(See GROUNDS; LETTINGS; TOILETS.)*

BULLYING

Hurting or persecuting weaker persons constitutes bullying. You need to be aware that we are all susceptible to bullying and that it is not just the province of the child. Adults can bully and be bullied... As head, you need to question the reasoning underlying any intimidating behaviour.

- What contributes to bullying tactics?
- What precipitates such behaviour?
- How do you recognise bullying?
- Can you distinguish between real bullying and simply inappropriate behaviour?

The term "bully" is all too often over-used and consequently evokes over-reaction! Conversely, if bullying is taking place, you must not let it persist in any *way*, *shape*, or *form*! Both bully and victim need your help and will benefit from the problem being addressed. Bullies come in all shapes and forms! One thing they share is an insecurity in coming to terms with themselves and in subsequently relating to others. A child's school experience can be damaged, sometimes irreparably, by being subjected to intimidating behaviour. Adults too, can have their working life adversely affected by the bullying tactics of colleagues.

How do you deal with such a phenomenon?
- Have an active whole-school behavioural policy, with clear sanctions for inappropriate behaviour and a reward system.
- Ensure that *all* children, staff, parents and governors have ownership of their behavioural policy.
- Initiate and implement an agreed Code of Conduct for all staff.
- Cultivate and nurture a caring ethos and philosophy *daily* throughout the school.
- Be confident in dealing with all undesirable behavioural traits.
- Never overlook or condone.
- Question your own behaviour and that of all your pupils and staff.
- Lead by example in your interactions with the whole community.

(*See DISCIPLINE; BEHAVIOUR.*)

BUSINESS

It could be argued that the 1988 Education Reform Act made it incumbent on you to run your school like a business. In taking on the responsibility for Local Management of Schools, you have to manage a budget.

This means that you have to make crucial decisions concerning:
- staffing
- buildings and grounds
- maintenance
- cleaning
- educational expenditure.

BUSINESS

You must remain in credit and not allow a deficit budget. In order to break even financially, you will have to make critical decisions.

Decisions that involve cost-cutting:

- reducing expenditure
- raising funds

You are totally accountable and must therefore be business-like.

As a business person, you will exercise the skills of:

- a capitalist
- an employer
- an entrepreneur
- a financier
- an industrialist
- an executive.

In running a successful school you need to be business-like. This will require being:

- efficient
- effective
- accountable
- methodical
- organised
- practical
- systematic.

You must evaluate:

- the aims of your establishment
- the needs of your establishment
- the means available to you
- your proposed ends.

You need to put into place systems that keep you constantly informed of all developments. You must learn to keep "your finger on the pulse" at all times, while using the skills of others.

You are the PROFESSIONAL.

You MANAGE.

You LEAD.

You are a BUSINESS PERSON.

You SUCCEED.

(See also MANAGEMENT.)

CARETAKERS

Caretakers are often a law unto themselves. Some are the salt of the earth and will do anything for you – others make the head's job look more like the labours of Hercules. Until quite recently, the name of the caretaker took pride of place on the school's name board, betokening formidable status and power.

But with devolved budgets, open enrolment and Ofsted, the role of caretakers has changed. They have to be managed effectively to ensure that your buildings and site are clean, safe and secure. Caretakers need training in cleaning and repairs. They need to be managers of plant, equipment and personnel. They also need to know that clean and efficiently run buildings attract new pupils and their parents.

For the new head, getting the caretaker on your side is a priority management objective. It may not appear in your Development Plan and it's probably better not to tell anyone what you're doing ... but it has to be done!

Start with checking that your caretaker has a current job description. Does it reflect the tasks that really need to be done? How many hours does your caretaker work and at what time are the breaks? Do the holiday breaks match with when you want the school closed? Can you find your caretaker in an emergency?

Does your caretaker have the necessary training in cleaning methods, use of machinery and supervision of cleaners to be effective? Does your caretaker feel valued by *you*?

We would recommend:

- daily or weekly meetings to check on the quality of cleaning, safety and security of your buildings

- a "snags book" kept in a prominent place to record minor maintenance jobs which need doing

- a mobile extension phone if your caretaker is elusive

- regular appraisal linked with training

- spot checks on toilets, playgrounds, boiler rooms.

Caretakers are often left to manage themselves and their time because their job is seen as different from that of teachers and administrative staff. It's not. Everyone is engaged in the same endeavour, which is about securing quality teaching and learning for children. A dirty or unsafe school undermines the work of everyone.

CHARISMA

Problems with personal power and image? Losing that knack for the well-timed *bon mot* to lift the spirits of the meals supervisors? Still wearing last year's frock from the Miss Selfridge Autumn Collection? Do people start talking about the weather when you're chairing meetings? Your charisma needs some attention!

Start with an appraisal of yourself. What do you look like? Attractive, well-groomed, confident and interesting? You should do because you're a head! People want you to be their leader and you have to show them you have style. Change your wardrobe. Buy those clothes you never dared to before. Have your hair styled differently. Swap your estate car for something foreign and noisy and get a sticker in the back window that says "Bungee jumpers do it with bands."

Next look at how you relate to people. How is your eye-contact? Do you have a firm handshake? When you ask someone to do something, do you say, "Er . . . would you mind doing this for me when you have time . . ?" or do you say, "I'd like you to do this for me. Please let me have it by nine tomorrow"?

And what about your intellect? Read any good books lately? Do you know your Vygotsky from your Fullan? Do you engage in stimulating debate in the staff room and challenge conventional wisdom? Some people are born charismatic, but for most ordinary mortals, we have to work at it.

CHARITIES

Charity collections can take up a considerable amount of time and cause their fair share of problems. The vast majority are run by honest and reasonable people. Schools are considered fair game by charities for a whole range of worthwhile causes and contribute hundreds of thousands of pounds every year. The major charities will make an appointment with you. You can control these easily. For other fund collectors, where appeals are made direct to the children through magazines or television, keeping control is quite difficult. Collections of silver paper, bottle tops, stamps, old tools, clothing and newspapers all need to managed by someone. And you need the space and time to do it. Schools are primarily about educating children. Acting as an unpaid accountant for a major charity or providing free warehouse facilities for mountains of unwashed bottle tops is not really your job.

One way to solve the problem is to decide which charities and collections you will support in the following year – and stick to it. You could sponsor one each term. For example, a national charity in the autumn, a local environmental one in the spring and perhaps a school-based sponsored activity in the summer. Tell your parents and governors in a newsletter, so that everyone has adequate warning. Parents and children could then decide which ones (if any) they want to support. You can then reluctantly decline requests to collect old wheelbarrows for Albania and aluminium cans to save the grasshopper.

CLEANERS

Do you consider your cleaners part of your staff? Are they valued, motivated and rewarded? If so, you probably don't have a problem to solve. If not, you will have to deal with a continual stream of complaints and frustrations. You will also have a building which is dirty and unwelcoming.

Start with job descriptions. Make clear the standards you expect. Ensure that the work expected can be done in the time allocated and that cleaners' workloads are fairly apportioned. Provide training in the use of machines and routines. Generate team spirit with tabards and overalls! Make sure that your caretaker supervises their work closely. Go round yourself from time to time to pick up problems and thank the cleaning staff for their work. Show a keen interest. Value suggestions on improving the quality. Spend money wisely on carpets, paint and furnishings which need the minimum of care.

Enlist the help of the children and staff with a "help them to help us" approach. Finally, don't overlook your cleaners when you are organising school events and celebrations. Everyone should be invited to concerts, school plays and PTA Beetle Drives! The greater the feeling of involvement in school life, the greater will be the commitment.

CLOCKS

The minimum length of the school week recommended by the Secretary of State is 21 hours for children at five, rising to 23.5 for eleven-year-olds. Schools are run to tight schedules to make sure the curriculum is covered and bad time-keeping will raise tensions among the staff and children. Accurate clocks are essential. The main problems are inaccurate settings when the hour changes in spring and autumn, lack of regular checks, and batteries!

When the hour goes forward or back, get your caretaker to adjust clocks on the Friday before the weekend. Exhausted teachers may not notice and rush home early in the spring. They get caught out in the autumn, picking up their children an hour late and arriving home to charred boeuf bourgignon, so lavishly prepared on the Thursday night. Make sure that your caretaker understands that walking around changing clocks actually takes time and that they shouldn't all be set to the same time. It has been known...

You can avoid problems with batteries by changing them every September. This may seem extravagant but those extra volts in February are a real boon. Make one of your clocks the "official one". This will give your school its own time zone and allow you to rule if a child, or member of staff, is late, or leaves early. There is a serious point here. If a child leaves late, or early, and is injured on the way home, you could be called to account.

COLLECTIONS

Collections for staff who are ill or leaving are usually no problem. Someone goes round with a tin, then buys the present and you make a flattering speech at the end of term. What happens when several people leave, all having given the same length of service but the amount collected for one is significantly less than the others? Do you subsidise the kitty from your own money or use the money collected as a general fund. Or do you simply spend what has been given for each person?

Rule number one has to be to protect the collector. You can't ask contributors to reveal what they have given. But if you do anticipate trouble, your collector could give a receipt note to each person. The money collected should be counted by another member of staff and then placed in the safe.

Rule number two is to safeguard relationships and respect the feelings of individuals. If an embarrassingly small amount has been collected, a large pot plant and an envelope containing store vouchers are a good way out.

Rule number three is to play safe with the gifts. Hair restorer, accurate watches, and lingerie are not diplomatic for the follicly challenged, tardy or straight-laced. Glasses, decanters, wheel-barrows, croquet sets and vulgar ornaments go down well.

In some secondary schools and larger primaries, the staff pay a contribution at the start of each year into a gift fund. You could do the same if you find collections problematic. The advantages are that there aren't frequent requests for money and the system saves time on collecting. The big advantage is that it doesn't become personalised. And at least when *you* leave you'll be sure to get you own contribution back.

COLLEGIALITY

The willingness of all staff to support and contribute in sharing reponsibility for whole-school development is an indication of a collegial approach in action.

Teachers committed to collegiality see the positive atmosphere in your school as the element most critical to its maintenance. They can derive strong personal and professional satisfaction from their involvement in, and contribution to, its continuation.

Your role as head is instrumental in developing a collegial approach. Knowing when to "lead" and when to "manage" is not easy. In order to empower others, it could be argued that the distinction must be exercised appropriately. In recognising the value of all staff contributing to school development, you need to acknowledge the importance of your role in monitoring activities.

Benefits of collegiality
- empowerment of staff
- commitment of all
- shared vision
- united responsiblity
- a common purpose and mission
- involvement of others in the decision-making process.

What is the collegial school?

It is one where your staff feed back suggestions for school-wide change and a corporate identity is developed. You will encourage an atmosphere where constructive criticism of each other's practice becomes a natural feature. Your staff will support and analyse each other's practice. You will share a common set of values. These will underpin your decision-making process and together you will achieve your aims.

The beneficiaries of collegiality will be:
- your pupils
- your staff
- YOU.

Consider:

In committing yourself to a collegial approach, you need to be secure in what you want for your school. You need to be secure in yourself! In advancing collegiality, you will be challenging your own power-base.

True collegiality will survive the departure of the head. . !

COMMUNICATION

In schools, breakdowns in communication cause more friction than arguments over philosophy or practice. Setting up the systems and channels for communication are your first responsibility. Making sure that they are used is your second.

At a basic level, inadequate communication over routine information, such as timetable changes or duty rotas, will cause frustration. But having incomplete systems for the development of policy and the dissemination of information is disastrous.

As a head you need to communicate *directly* with different groups. The most important ones are obviously your staff, the children, your governing body and parents. But communication is two-way: it's essential that you are accessible to everyone.

You can minimise the potential for communications breakdown.

• Make sure that every member of your staff knows their responsibilities and to whom they are accountable.

• Agree on a structure of meetings for the different groups who lead, manage and deliver the curriculum in your school. Specify intervals at which groups need to meet.

• Meet regularly with support assistants, secretaries, meals supervisors and your caretaker.

• Agendas for all meetings, apart from those dealing with confidential personal issues involving staff or children, need to be within the domain of the whole organisation.

• Make sure that all meetings are minuted and filed for reference. This allows everyone to know what is going on, even though they may not be directly involved. You can also check that decisions have been acted upon. It also allows you, the head, to keep your finger on the pulse and decide which meetings you need to attend.

• Use every opportunity to communicate *directly* with individuals and groups. This will enhance your visible, "hands-on" management style. Take time to talk. Listen carefully to what people say.

• Use as many forms of communication as you can but choose the right medium for the message. Minor changes in routine can be communicated by note or on a noticeboard. But delicate staffing issues or personal matters need the direct one-to-one approach.

• Make it a rule that you see all letters before they are sent out.

Finally, remember that anything which comes directly from you has high value. A phone call or card when someone is ill or the handwritten note to a concerned parent, demonstrate not only that you care but that you are well-informed. Make use of these opportunities but be economical with them. And beware of those casual off-the-cuff remarks in unguarded moments or the attempt at humour which goes sadly wrong. Nothing travels faster than bad news; and the bigger the gaffe the more people who get to hear about it.

COMMUNITY

There are a variety of problems which devolve on schools from the wider community. In some areas, it is almost impossible to generate any interest in school. Parents may either be too busy working and coping with the pressures of modern life, or, may they feel that education is the job of the school and be content simply to hand over their children. In other areas, particularly the more affluent suburbs, you may be swamped by the demands to take part in community functions. Or you may have legions of well-meaning parents only too willing to help in the classroom and organise social events. They take time and effort to manage.

At the other extreme, you may work in a school which is a constant target for vandals, neighbours, parents or the local press.

One thing is sure. Most schools go through a continual cycle of gaining and losing good relations with their communities and heads have to work at it all the time. You do have influence over some of the factors – but not all. For example, a school which is next door to a pub or take-away food shop, may find its reputation affected by the number of fist-fights on a Saturday night or by the rubbish thrown into the playground every night.

If your school is under attack in the press or from a small group, remember that they are unlikely to represent more than a few disgruntled souls. The chances are that the more time you spend on it, the more you risk prolonging the trouble.

What you can do to maintain sound relations with your public depends on your school and your community. But it is worth considering the following:

- Open your doors: make your public aware of the good work you do. Invite in community groups to your assemblies, concerts or sports afternoons.

- Set up a community group. Encourage them to organise functions – and not just for generating funds.

- It is a fact that buildings that are in use by the local community are vandalised less. Encourage the use of your buildings in the evenings, at weekends and during the holidays.

- Celebrate your school's successes publicly. Develop your contacts on the local paper.

- Build up a register of parents and friends willing to share some time in school. Invite them to mince pies and coffee at Christmas or send a personal card of thanks at the end of the year.

- If you have co-options to fill on your governing body, choose those who have links with social, cultural or interest groups within your community.

Finally, make every child and adult connected with your school an ambassador. Everyone likes to be associated with good news. Communities which have vibrant, well-run and exciting schools will feel good about sharing in that success.

CONFERENCES

Heads receive mail from a variety of sources about conferences on everything from Personal Effectiveness to Ofsted and Assessment to Curriculum Planning. Do you pay the conference fee from your GEST budget, consider it an investment for your school . . . or feel that you are playing hookey and worry all day that the school will burn down?

Heads have an entitlement to professional development. Indeed, without it you will gradually ossify into one of those dinosaurs you vowed you'd never become before your got the job!

Make it a golden rule that you will go to at least two conferences each year. Not only will you come back refreshed and full of new ideas but you will also have had the opportunity to network with other heads. You might also be able to eat a decent lunch without being called on to sort out playground squabbles or find out who has flooded the toilets.

Your staff will benefit too. By leaving them, you show that you trust them. When you return they'll be pleased to see you and hear how hard you had to work. Share what you learned with them at the earliest opportunity. If they didn't notice you were away in the first place, then you really have got a problem!

CONFLICT

You cannot avoid conflict. But you can use it to advantage. Conflict is a powerful tool in decision-making. In fact, it could be argued that the visionary head can even use conflict to advantage. Remember that conflict can be developmental and is a dynamic force if managed creatively.

As headteacher, you need to need to come to terms with the fact that your school is unlikely to be staffed by superpeople! You need to make the most of the staff you have. Don't waste time wishing for Utopia. Use all situations to maximum advantage in gaining ground in your role. Try to be flexible and ultimately creative in turning negative situations to positive gain.

Since Marx, conflict theory has been a significant part of sociological analysis, but there has been a notable revival of interest in recent years. Within all schools there will be various interest groups, each with its own particular goals. The enlightened head will manipulate any conflict, whilst observing the methods by which each group gains advantage over the other.

Conflicting interests can be managed eventually to form a common cause for the school, or be contrived to meet the head's "hidden agenda" (which ideally will be in tune with the former!).

Be alert at all times to mood and atmosphere and try to be one step ahead. Never admit defeat and learn to view all situations favourably!

Conflict needs to be bravely confronted and managed with confidence, openly or otherwise ... Remember, like most things in headship, conflict management can EVEN BE FUN!

CONKERS

Who can deny the simple pleasures of the annual conker season? Caretakers can. Playgrounds are littered with the shells of the defeated, making the surface slippery, dangerous and untidy. Teachers tear their hair out settling disputes which take up valuable teaching time. Meals supervisors threaten resignation or industrial action.

Our advice is to go with the tide. Set out a simple set of rules which are easily enforced. For example:

- Declare a conker season with a set finish and end.

- Insist that all conkers be bored and drilled at home, which stops vicious marlin spikes and skewers in trouser pockets.

- Insist that all pieces of conker are picked up by victor and vanquished.

- Reserve an area for conker fights only, with a bucket for the remains.

- Get the children to show their best examples in Assembly and even draw up a league for inter-class championships.

Finally, have a go yourself! Get the biggest conker you can find. Soak it in vinegar and cook it for 15 minutes at 160° Centigrade. For a world-beater, you can coat it with yacht varnish. Your status will go up enormously whether you win or lose. And don't forget that the anniversary of the Battle of Hastings falls on 14 October, right in the middle of the conker season. You can wax lyrical on conkers and conquerors . . .

CONTRACTORS

The local management of schools has put a new slant on the relationship that heads have with contractors. Placing orders and holding the purse strings yourself brings a greater bargaining power.

Most contractors welcome this. There is an opportunity to provide a more personal, better-quality service and to negotiate prices directly with you. You have the advantage of specifying exactly the work you require and when it should be done. Contractors see schools as their bread and butter. The work is regular and payment reliable. Most schools use local contractors who are used to working in the school environment. They can usually be relied upon to work with you to avoid disruption to the school routine. So what are the problems?

As in many things, the main problems arise through poor communication. You can reduce these in a number of ways.

- Use contractors who are approved: your LEA should keep a list to help you.

- Stick to the agreement that you have with your governing body about authorising work. Most governing bodies need to be consulted if work exceeds a given figure.

- When you place an order, make sure it is on the basis of a *quotation* and not an *estimate* and always confirm this in writing.

- Check that the contractors you use are registered for paying tax or you may find that you become liable when you have an audit of your finances.

- Specify when the work should be done, e.g. a holiday or after school.

- Make sure that anyone working on your site is signed in and that your caretaker keeps an eye on them.

- Only agree to pay after you, or a nominated person, has checked that the job has been done.

Contracts which are arranged on your behalf for work paid for by the LEA can cause problems. Grounds maintenance, heating and electrical systems and structural work are good examples. Contractors who turn up out of the blue to turn off your boiler or dismantle a temporary classroom should be turned away. Non-urgent work can always be re-scheduled for a holiday or weekend when it is safer for the children – and easier for the contractor.

CONTRACTS (FINANCE)
Contracts with suppliers for services and equipment are an important element of budget planning. You can avoid problems by following the golden rules.

- Are you sure you actually need the service or equipment in the first place?

- Make sure that your governing body approves the expenditure in principle.

- Contact your LEA personnel for lists of approved suppliers.

- Take at least three written quotations. Estimates are not worth the paper they're written on. Check that your budget will stand the costs. Contracts for site maintenance and cleaning will probably be for three years, with an option to revise the specification annually. Costs may rise year on year.

- Other services for copiers, computers and fax machines could be for up to five years. Although the charges may remain constant, the equipment may be obsolete in months. Will you have the option to upgrade, or be stuck with a dinosaur in your office?

- Make sure your governors approve the best deal and that the decision is minuted.

- Go through the contract with a fine toothcomb. Does it really fulfil your requirements? When you are sure, ask your chair of governors, or an LEA officer to check again.

- When you sign on the dotted line, have a governor with you. Check the fine print: refuse if you're not happy. Always check that what you sign is bona fide. Sadly, it's not unknown for carbon paper to be slipped under a top copy, literally giving the impression that you've signed the one underneath, which of course, will cost considerably more!

If, despite your best intentions, you are landed with a lemon, or your budget will not stand the expense, do something about it! It may or may not be your responsibility. If it is, say so. If you've been duped, don't get angry, get even. Let your LEA and your governors know. Contact the MD of the company. Seek advice.

CONTRACTS (STAFF)

Contracts for staff are either permanent or temporary. Key positions, deputies and those with management or core curriculum responsibilities are almost always permanent.

Maternity cover appointments and those to cover long-term illness are usually temporary because there is already a permanent post-holder.

Problems arise over SNS posts and other staff, when budget constraints may reduce staffing levels in the following financial year. You and your governors need to weigh up the pros and cons of a temporary appointment.

Contracts which can cause the greatest difficulty are internal temporary promotions. Beware the consequences! Expectations and status are raised and it is very difficult for a teacher who has been acting deputy for two terms suddenly to give up the status and responsibility. The money will have been useful too. Moving aside for the new encumbent takes a high degree of professional self-discipline. You may end up losing more than you gain.

CRISIS

A crisis in school is beyond the normal round of day-to-day problems. By its nature, a crisis is a sudden, unforeseen event which permanently affects the life of the school and those who are caught up in it. Most heads will at some time have contemplated how they will react when faced with a crisis. The sudden death of a child or member of staff, or an accident when children are away on a visit, are possibilities that heads have to cope with. Everyone will look to you to take the lead and it will probably be the most testing time, emotionally and professionally, that you will ever have to face.

If you can, try to think ahead and develop a contingency plan before a crisis happens.

- Set up effective communications with your LEA, parents, staff, police and rescue agencies.
- Make sure that you have LEA Emergency Procedures documents at hand, including names and phone numbers of key people, e.g. Chief Education Officer, Press Officer, County or Borough Solicitor.
- Talk to your governors and agree procedures.
- Make sure that your roll list with addresses and phone numbers is up to date.

We would recommend reading *Wise Before the Event* by William Yule and Anne Gold (Calouste Gulbenkian Foundation, 1993).

DEADLINES

Meeting deadlines is about doing things on time. You might have agreed this time with someone else or have no choice over when the task has to be done. You also set your own deadlines. And they mean as much, for you, as any externally-set targets!

Meeting deadlines is about:
- getting yourself organised
- being in charge of your time
- balancing your needs, goals, and professional and personal values
- interacting positively.

Meeting deadlines is about *you* taking charge of your time! It is about prioritising your time. It is about learning to recognise what is important to YOU. Meeting deadlines is about TAKING control. Meeting deadlines is about REMAINING in control.

Dealing with deadlines:
- Do not commit yourself to anything you cannot deliver.
- Do not commit yourself unless you really have to!
- Schedule your day.
- Recognise what is within your control.
- Prioritise.
- Set your own goals.
- Know what is "non-negotiable" and "negotiable".
- Plan your time in a manner to suit YOU.
- In meeting the needs of others, protect YOURSELF.
- Delegate.

You will have deadlines but most can be within your control. You can be pro-active rather than re-active.

In taking charge of deadlines, you will use your skills of managing time, people and yourself.

In meeting deadlines, you will acquire the reward of maximising your time and even enjoying it!

DEARING

After years of programmed uncertainty, and just when we seemed to be coming to terms with what we were doing, what happens? A postman is given the task of re-evaluating the National Curriculum! Sir Ron Dearing led a group of notables, the outcome of which was the Dearing Report (1993).

What is the significance of this report to you as head?
- You need to read it!
- Become acquainted with its contents.
- Evaluate its significance.
- Decide what changes, if any, you need to make in delivering the curriculum.
- Consider how you are going to manage any change.

DEATH

Dealing with, or responding to, a death in your school is a dreaded experience. In any event the cessation of life is difficult to come to terms with. Any death in your school will affect you in your role as head. But before you can help others, you must recognise and cope with your own emotions. You may well have to handle the death of:

A member of staff
You will have to consider the feelings and emotions of children, colleagues, parents and pupils.

The parent of a child
A pupil left motherless or fatherless will be bereft. Other children will be frightened and confused.

A child
Bereavement of any kind is painful. The death of a child may well be the hardest phenomenon of all to deal or cope with. Everyone in your school will be thrown off-balance. All will express their confusion and disarray in various ways.

How do you respond?
- Deal with your own feelings
- Allow yourself to express your emotions.
- Put the needs of others first.
- Allow others to express their sentiments.
- Be prepared for a variety of reactions.

- Be brave.
- Plan some time (circle/assembly/memorial) when those who need to, can express their emotions.

"Death is . . . really a change: a migration of the soul from one place to another." (Plato, *Apology*, 41.)

DEFAMATION

You may have to deal with problems that arise from an alleged defamation. This could be slander or libel. Those who seek to lower someone in the estimation of right-thinking members of society by making a false statement, and then communicate it to a third party, could be challenged in law. With slander, the aggrieved party will have to prove that damage has been caused. Libel is the permanent form, either written or recorded in some way, but proof of damage is not necessarily required.

It is possible, but unlikely, that a pupil or parent might feel defamed by a teacher. More often it is teachers who complain of being defamed.

Education is a matter of public interest. If the person making a statement amounting to a comment about the quality of education provision, believes it to be based upon fact, it will be difficult to challenge in law. If the statement amounting to a comment about the quality of educational provision is true, or substantially true, this will also be an adequate defence. If the defamation is unintentional and an apology is offered, it is unlikely that any better remedy could be secured. Even personalised allegations can be defended, though false, if made only to someone who has a proper interest in receiving them, for example, to you as head, to the governors or the LEA. A claim can be made in these circumstances by proving that the allegation was malicious.

Pursuing a case for defamation is an exhausting business. Litigation is very expensive and few cases reach the courts. If you feel you have a case, contact your LEA legal department and your professional association.

DELEGATION

How good are you at trusting others? Can you devolve authority and allow others to take charge? With all that headship entails it is impossible to do everything yourself.

Even if you wish it, you cannot be all of the following at the same time:

- expert
- initiator
- innovator
- the one who implements.

You may be some, or all, of these things; but it would be wise to question the validity, wisdom or feasibility of attempting to exercise these skills constantly.

What you will gain if you try to achieve the impossible:
- an under-developed school
- an uninspired staff
- under-achieving children and staff
- compliance
- dissatisfaction
- burn-out.

What will you gain if you delegate?
- support
- empowered individuals
- fulfilment
- commitment
- sharing of vision and purpose.

The realisation that you cannot do everything yourself can be quite a personal revelation. Why spend time doing things others can do as well, if not better? There are some tasks that only you as head can do. These are the things that you need to get on with!

In delegating, you must achieve the right mix of *challenge* and *support*. Too much support and pressure can be stultifying and detrimental to individuals and any team cohesion. As a shrewd and astute administrator you can work to get the balance correct.

DEPUTY HEADTEACHER
The peculiar world of the deputy head teacher demands the ability to perform like a circus juggler, shouldering a whole range of responsibilities and tasks without turning a hair. The time to do all the work and usually teach full-time, is impossible. Yet still committed and energetic teachers fling themselves into the fray! Teachers who want to be heads almost always have to serve as deputies if they want the excitement of running a school.

Deputies always have to be recognised as superb practitioners who know their craft and demonstrate it. They also need to have sound interpersonal skills to deal with the sensitive and serious issues that can arise in any school. Now in the 1990s we also expect our deputies to have a range of managerial and financial skills. Knowing the curriculum inside out is essential and this grows with experience and training. Making a success of the other aspects of deputy headship demands specific training. Deputies play a pivotal role in the success of the primary school, working in partnership with the head and governors. A poorly motivated, inadequate or incompetent deputy will undermine the quality of the work of your school.

What do you do, as head?
Start with an audit of your deputy's skills and experience. In which areas would some professional development help? Is your deputy's job description still relevant and when did you last review it together? What is the difference between the workloads of your deputy and the next most senior person? Do you really delegate to your deputy and do you give them feedback on how they are doing? If you are not, you may not be making the most of your investment. Talk, but above all listen, to your deputy and work out how you can manage your respective responsibilities. Aim for clear descriptions of the tasks to be done – and how they will be evaluated. Talk through plans for the next move in the career stakes and how to build up skills and experience to add to your deputy's c.v.

Most deputies are solid, reliable and hard working – but they can soon be disillusioned and go off the boil if they feel unloved! Giving your deputy more responsibility and greater recognition may actually be a solution to the mid-career blues. After all, those who have a great deal of work to do, never have time to complain, do they?

DIET

Your diet is very likely to become an unhealthy one. Healthy drinking and eating habits often suffer in headship. Your falling energy level is replenished at intervals throughout the working day by fistfuls of custard-creams and cups of coffee.

Yet we are all aware of the basic guidelines for a healthy diet:

- reducing intake of saturated fats
- keeping blood pressure low by cutting down on salt
- avoiding too many sugar products
- eating more fibre
- increasing daily intake of fresh food.

You will feel better and more able to deal with difficult situations, if you monitor your diet.

Look after yourself!

(See HEALTH.)

DIRECTED TIME

The teacher's job has never been confined to the pupil day but until 1988 there was no clear definition of the hours teachers could be required to work. There is still no exact definition but we do now have directed time.

The whole job of teaching according to a list of duties can be required – reasonably. That part of it when the full-time teacher is at the head's disposal is confined to 1265 hours per year spread over 195 days of which 190 days are days when the school is open to pupils.

The hours and days are hours and days of availability for work under the head's direction. There is no requirement that every hour must be called upon in every case. Indeed it is part of a headteacher's responsibility to achieve a reasonable distribution of overall workload among the teaching staff. The essential point is that directed time should be used purposefully, at the head's discretion.

If you are wise, you will plan and outline the use of this time at the beginning of each school year. Staff will respect clarification of what is expected of them. They can then plan their time accordingly. Teachers' unions also prefer their members to know where they stand.

A magnanimous head is not one who seems to demand little of the staff but expects them to use their time for meetings or such-like at little or no notice! A harmonious team will not be created by expecting people to answer to such whims. They will not work the hours expected of them ungrudgingly, with little or no forward planning.

Use directed time creatively, to the advantage of your pupils, staff and school. If you manage this, you might benefit too!

DISASTERS

Unfortunately disasters happen frequently and although you would prefer to comfort yourself with the thought that disasters will always happen elsewhere, your school could at some time be affected. You may feel that you are tempting fate if you even start to consider how you might react if a cataclysmic event befell! On the other hand, it might be worth questioning whether you could reduce any impact if you do think ahead. You will not "will" a catastrophe to happen by just thinking about it. But you might just assist others, and cope better yourself, if you are prepared in some way.

What can you do?
- identify likely critical incidents
- develop a contingency plan with governors and staff
- know whom to contact in the case of an emergency
- define roles and responsibilities
- be contactable.

In the case of a tragedy, you need to:
- identify immediate tasks
- inform others
- deal with the media
- deal with those most affected

- continue with normal routine while acknowledging any disastrous effects
- enlist the support of outside professionals.

For the security of all children and staff, it is important to maintain some form of normality. However, do allow for people to express their emotions and be prepared for these to be manifest in various ways and differing situations. A de-briefing meeting and/or a service of some kind needs to be considered as appropriate. Whatever the problem, you want to nurture an atmosphere of confidence, trust and security for all concerned.

But what about you?

You must allow yourself to express your feelings in some way. Only if you do this will you be able to support others in a way that will really help them. *(See ACCIDENTS.)*

DISCIPLINE

Whether you like it or not, as head you are a disciplinarian. You are responsible for the discipline of your pupils and that of your staff. Their basic conduct is condoned, or not, by you. All establishments are expected to exhibit a certain level of orderliness. Individuals, adults or children are required to develop self-control in order to live harmoniously together.

As part of your role you have to regulate all behaviour in your school. This means that you have to control that behaviour to a lesser or greater degree as appropriate. You will aim to nurture and develop a favourable philosophy and ethos, and together with your staff and children, generally to interact positively together. It is when this does *not* happen that you have to reprove in some way! This means that you are taking a form of disciplinary action.

In the case of staff this will be evoking the formal disciplinary procedure. But unless the conduct to be reproved is so serious as to justify resorting to extreme measures, it will be normal to adopt one or more of the common disciplinary courses of action such as:

- a one-to-one chat
- a more formal and serious discussion including the recording of statements of witnesses to an incident

- offering support to overcome identified causes of a problem.

In the case of pupils this will be:
- according to the sanctions clearly outlined in your behavioural policy
- in rare and extreme cases, to exclude for a given period.

In taking any form of disciplinary action, you need to be cautious and measured. You are accountable for your interactions and must not therefore jeopardise any procedures. Ensure that you do everything according to "the book". As always, if you put the interests of your pupils first, you will succeed even in this, the most unenviable task in headship.

(See also PUNISHMENT; BEHAVIOUR; BULLYING.)

DISCRIMINATION

To discriminate is to single out a particular group or individual for special favour or disfavour. If you do this you exclude some individuals or groups from certain experiences. Some discrimination such as favouring good behaviour against bad behaviour is of course entirely proper. Unjustifiable discrimination is unacceptable. It can be intentional or unintentional, direct or indirect. Indirect discrimination occurs when an obstacle is placed in the way of an individual or group affecting that individual or group more than others.

In your influential position as head, you would be wise to examine whether you could ever be guilty of unfair discriminatory practice!

If your governing body has a well-planned selection procedure, it is unlikely that you will appoint a person unsuited or unqualified for a vacant post in your school. You need to be conscious in order to avoid making assumptions about others. Such behaviour leads to prejudice, when you prejudge on inadequate facts.

Discrimination takes many forms:
- racism
- against religious groups
- on the basis of gender

- political
- on grounds of life-style
- on grounds of dress.

In your position as head you act as a powerful role model and set the tone for tolerance, understanding and positive action. You need to challenge others if you suspect discriminatory practice. If you fail to so do, you will be seen to collude and oppress. Never avoid your responsibility to do something about institutional oppression if it applies to your school, or the wider community which you can influence.

If you empathise with those who are being discriminated against you will gain confidence in combatting such unacceptable behaviour. *(See BULLYING; EQUAL OPPORTUNITIES; PROTECTION; RACISM; SEXISM; SEXUAL HARASSMENT.)*

DISPLACEMENT ACTIVITY

Displacement activity is behaviour that typically occurs in times of stress or conflict. How often, in your role as head, could your behaviour be regarded as irrelevant to the situation with which you are, or should be, dealing? You need continually to question whether or not you are using your time to good effect. Are you in fact, consciously or unconsciously, avoiding issues or tasks that can be addressed? If the answer is "Yes", why is this the case? If you are too easily distracted, is it a healthy diversion or an obstacle to concentration?

What can you do?

- Recognise the difference between displacement activity and unhealthy or healthy distractions.
- Evaluate your use of time.
- Question your efficiency and effectiveness.
- Be realistic about what you can achieve in any given time.
- Set yourself clear achievable targets.
- Have a beginning and ending to your working day.
- Cultivate a hobby.
- Allow yourself treats, no matter how insignificant your achievement.

- Question whether or not you are getting sufficient exercise.
- Try to analyse why you are avoiding the issue.
- Look at your diet and sleep pattern.

Above all, be realistic in your assessment of yourself and others.

DISPLAYS

Displays – on wall, noticeboard or table-top – reveal and make visible the practice of your school. Displays will make an impression on those who come into your school. They should make an impression on those who spend their daily time within your organisation. You would hope that all impression would be favourable . . . act as a stimulus . . . evoke a positive sensation in the viewer. In reality this is not always the case, because successful display requires:

- a measure of artistic appreciation and ability
- time
- appropriate lettering to complement display
- a rolling programme of change.

All staff will have different strengths and yet it is essential that all develop their display techniques and maximise their potential in this important area.

How is this done?
- Encourage your art coordinator and other artistic colleagues to organise display workshops,for all staff, to illustrate simple ways of developing effective display.
- Ensure that display is integral in the planning process.
- Challenge ineffective display appropriately and assertively.
- Encourage others to do likewise.
- Never allow spelling mistakes in lettering; calmly insist that changes are made as soon as possible.

In considering the display in your school, do come to an agreement with staff about the balance of pupil and staff input. If the children do the lettering make sure that this is obvious to others. Poor lettering can devalue an otherwise effective display. Too much adult input in display can also leave pupil potential unrealised. Encourage staff to appreciate and subsequently capitalise on the impact of display. Exploited creatively, it can be a tremendous teaching tool and a marketing asset for your school. We all like to be in pleasant and interesting surroundings, so never underestimate the influence of display. Do not allow display to become the wallpaper in your school!

DOGS

Dogs can be a real menace to schools. A stray on the playground just as the whistle is about to go, will excite and unsettle the children. Even the smallest dog may frighten some children and adults, jumping up or even biting them.

A more common problem concerns dog-fouling in the school grounds – but particularly where children play. Every year some children lose their sight as a direct result of disease contracted through dog excrement. With such an obvious risk to the children's health, you and the Governing Body have the legal responsibility to do something about it. Under the Education Reform Act, Governing Bodies of LEA-maintained schools are responsible for health and safety.

We would recommend that you take steps to:
- erect signs at entrances telling owners that dogs are not permitted
- get your caretaker to check fences regularly and close the gates once the children are in
- cover jumping pits and renew sand regularly
- write to owners who you know are exercising dogs on your site
- enlist the support of your parents and governors by raising the issue.
- confront those who ignore the above!

DRESS

Heads often have to make judgements on dress: concerning both children and, sometimes, staff. Your school's prospectus should give clear guidance for parents on appropriate school wear. If uniform is expected, then the prospectus should say so. But in LEA-maintained schools you may be on dangerous ground if you adopt a rigid stance. Fundamentally, you should try to be reasonable. Parents who have cultural or philosophical reasons for differing over the choice of their children's school wear should be accommodated. Whatever your personal views, you are unlikely to win an argument on taste grounds, and even if you do, there may be a smouldering resentment which will manifest itself in some other way.

However, you have every right to object to clothing which could offend others, or be a hazard. For example, T-shirts with dubious slogans, voluminous shorts or micro-skirts, could be considered unsuitable for the classroom and playground not only because they might offend, but also because they might lead to accidents while the children are at work and play. Studs and rings in ears or noses may be fashionable, but must be removed for PE, Drama and Dance.

Commenting on staff dress is potentially disastrous. The odd remark, even in jest, can be misconstrued. It will reduce the professional standing of both you and your colleague and at worst lead to allegations of harassment. The best solution is to leave well alone and set the highest standards yourself. If you do feel that a member of staff is untidy or dirty, there will be an underlying cause. He or she may be depressed or unwell and you should try to find out. But you also have a duty to point this out assertively.

DRUGS ADMINISTRATION

Staff and pupils will be prescribed drugs to alleviate poor conditions of health. You will be wise, therefore, to consider a whole-school approach to the administration of drugs.

You might agree the following can be administered at school:
- short-term antibiotics
- both short-term and long-term medication
- long-term medication only.

To agree to give short-term medication can be an administrative problem within your school. You would do well to put this responsibility back to parents. You can make provision for them to come into school to administer the medication themselves or to work out the dosage to suit the school day. If you do not, however, agree to administer long-term medication, you may well be disadvantaging pupils from accessing the curriculum. In all cases administration of medicines should be strictly according to procedures approved in writing by a qualified medical practitioner and clearly made known to parents. Complex procedures or procedures involving personal privacy should only be undertaken by suitably trained staff members and only with their agreement.

Whatever your approach, have you:
- considered your legal responsibilities?
- obtained signed parental approval?
- agreed and formulated a Drugs Policy, involving all stake holders?

DRUG MISUSE
Drugs can be:
- medicines
- poisons
- remedies
- narcotics
- "dope".

A drug is something that you put into your body and that affects you in some way. The effect can have a positive or negative reaction.

Drugs can:
- anaesthetize
- deaden
- stupefy
- lift
- cure.

Drug misuse is an educational issue. Pupils, including those in primary schools, are likely to be exposed to the effects and influences of drug misuse in the wider community. Each school therefore has a responsibility to consider its response to drug misuse, working in partnership with health and social services, the police and other agencies. A pro-active drugs policy, which promotes a better understanding of drugs and their misuse amongst the whole school community will help ensure a considered and proportionate response to issues as they arise. (See DFE circular 4/95 "Drug Prevention and Schools".)

Be alert to signs of inappropriate or excessive drug taking in adults and children such as:
- tiredness

- lethargy
- lack of pride in appearance
- inability to concentrate
- reduction in appetite
- over/under-reaction to situations
- sudden mood change.

Children are vulnerable targets for the introduction of drug-taking. Beware, however, in the presentation of drugs education, of the "glorification" of drugs. Emphasising the problems might just attract some young people.

What about staff?

If you suspect drug misuse/abuse or notice any detrimental effects, you *must* react; you must take some form of action! The welfare of your pupils could be at risk and their interests must always come first.

Nicotine is a drug, but it is legal. However, your school would be a healthier place for all concerned if it was a designated 'No Smoking' zone.

EDUCATIONAL PSYCHOLOGISTS

Does your educational psychologist give you the support you need? Do you have enough professional time from them for working with children and for talking with teachers and parents? The chances are that you don't. But it is essential that you develop a sound working relationship with your psychologist if you are to provide the best possible support for children with special needs and your staff.

- Remember that you, your staff and parents know individual children far better than any visiting specialist can – however well qualified they may be in assessment and observation.
- Be well prepared for your EP. Documentation is essential for monitoring the progress of children with special needs. Know what you want to achieve and stick with it. Keep to the timing of your programme and write everything up afterwards.

Finally, don't forget that your EP will be trained in a range of skills that will be useful to you. Problems in the playground at lunchtimes may have a startlingly obvious cause to the trained eye. There may be features of your building or daily routines which generate tension among staff or children. Your colour schemes or furnishings may be undermining the calm and purposeful backdrop you need for a quality learning environment. And don't forget that your EP may be helpful in supporting teachers with problems of discipline, and staff or children who have been bereaved.

EDUCATION WELFARE OFFICERS

EWOs need to feel that they are part of your team. They should be able to recognise your shcool as a place where children come first. Developing a working relationship based upon a knowledge of your children and their needs is essential for a successful partnership. With troubled, abused or truanting children, you need all the help you can get.

Communicate with your EWO regularly and effectively – not just when you have problems. Make them feel they have a stake in your school and that you value the work they do.

ELECTIONS

You will experience various elections in your role as head. In your involvement you must be careful to ensure that you conduct yourself with integrity and dignity.

You will facilitate elections for:
- parent governors
- teacher governors
- PTA/Friends committee.

In so doing, ensure that you follow all outlined procedures carefully. To overlook or ignore any procedural aspect will be to your detriment. No matter how frustrating or time-consuming, never take short cuts. The whole process will be deemed to be null and void if any impropriety is discovered. The effect this would have on your image speaks for itself! Despite the fact that you may have a personal preference in an election concerning your school, you must not display this in any way. Do not be tempted to use your status in influencing potential voters . . . You might well get away with it once, or even twice, but not a third time! Allow people to make up their own minds and trust in their judgement.

Party political elections
Even though you may have strong political views, your role as head precludes you from imposing your political views on pupils, staff and parents. The law requires political balance in teaching. In the event of council or national Government elections you will be wise to respect the choice of others, even if this is abhorrent to you. To remain quiet about your own choice might well be in your interest. People will probably anyway be able to detect your political persuasion by your value-system, your philosophy and life code. Why expose yourself to potential ridicule or alienation by stating what you have no obligation or need to reveal? On the other hand, you may wish to be subtle. If it is that important to you and you feel that you can get away with it, go ahead!

"Dummy" elections
It can be invaluable experience for a variety of good educational reasons, for pupils to take part in "dummy" elections. You will be wise, however, to discuss and agree the boundaries with your staff before any such elections take place. Elections of any kind are contentious and you need to be careful not to create unnecessary problems for yourself. You do not want to be put into a position where accusations can be made of politically influencing your pupils. Determine just what your aim is, in undertaking any election process.

ENVIRONMENT
The quality of the exterior environment within your school boundary has a direct effect upon the lives of those within it. School grounds which are badly maintained, dirty and unsafe will make the children and staff feel insecure and undervalued: discipline and achievements will suffer. Solving problems with the environment needs a long-term plan of action.

Start by checking that everything that *should* be done *is* being done. Who is responsible for clearing litter? Is it in your caretaker's job description? Does your caretaker have the right equipment to do the job? Do you have enough bins and places to store rubbish? How about hiring a skip at the end of term and getting rid of all the mess?

Who has the contract to maintain your grounds? Check through the specification. Are the shrubs and flower beds receiving the care they need? External decoration is one area of maintenance which has been cut by many LEAs. A school which looks shabby will deter prospective parents. If yours needs a facelift and the LEA can't or won't pay, it might be worth finding the money to have the key areas done.

Give some thought to reducing maintenance and security costs in the future. Judicious planting of thorny hedges near fences and gates will deter trespassers and encourage everyone to stick to the paths. The careful positioning of low fencing and path edges will save grassed areas from being worn away.

Check that the signposts in your grounds are accurate and clear. If they are a target for the graffiti artist, reposition and renew them.

Above all, your exterior environment should be an outdoor classroom. It should be attractive, welcoming and full of interest where children feel secure to take part in a range of activities.

EQUAL OPPORTUNITIES

LEAs have responsibilities under the Education Act 1944, the Race Relations Act 1976 and the Sex Discrimination Act 1976. These Acts are to make sure that pupils and employees are not discriminated against on race or sex grounds. LEAs have policy statements which you and your Governing Body should stick to if you are to avoid challenges in law.

With open enrolment and the increased powers of Governing Bodies in recruitment and redundancy, it is the head as manager who is in the front line to ensure fair play.

By law, no pupil may be the subject of discrimination. If a complaint is received, it will come to you first. It may then be referred to the Governing Body and to the LEA. If there is no solution, the Secretary of State has a period of time to rule on the case and may direct the Governing Body to overturn a decision. County Courts may also become involved, but only after the Secretary of State has had two months to consider the case.

You can reduce the risks of contravening legislation where pupils are concerned by:

- ensuring equal entitlement to the whole curriculum, including daily collective worship, religious education and extra-curricular activities;

- applying standards of dress and behaviour which recognise the differences between cultures and religions;

- ensuring that resources, benefits and services are available to all children;

- taking care that pupils are not discriminated against by the application of your school's charging policy.

Complaints about discrimination on staffing issues usually revolve around recruitment procedures, conditions of employment, discipline and grievance, or redundancy.

- Make sure that your advertisements comply with the law.

- Draw up your criteria for posts carefully and refer to them throughout the process from receipt of applications, through short-listing, to appointment. Be explicit to candidates and ensure that the appointing panels are properly briefed.

- Agree on the questions for interview and stick to them. This is particularly important for governors who may be tempted to ask inappropriate questions.

- Provide assessment proformas for panels. Decisions will be objective and based on evidence. Keep all papers and notes in case there is a challenge.

- Offer de-briefing to the unsuccessful candidates.

- Make sure that internal candidates are treated in the same way as external ones.

- Redundancy and grievance procedures are complex and emotive. Give your staff all the information that you can and welcome the help of union representatives. Conduct the procedure to the letter and follow the advice of your LEA.

If there is a challenge, you must be able to prove you have acted fairly and openly. The biggest casualties are relationships and the effect upon morale. Prove that you and the Governing Body have acted with unimpeachable integrity and you stand a better chance of limiting damage.

(See DISCRIMINATION, RACISM, SEXISM, REDUNDANCY.)

EXCURSIONS

Day visits and residential excursions are an essential part of children's educational experience. However, for the head they are a potential source of worry. Parents and teachers have become more aware of the risks following the media coverage of accidents to children and young people. Governors and heads are accountable not just for the safety of the children, but to ensure that each excursion has an explicit educational purpose. There is an issue of equal entitlement when parents are asked to make "voluntary" contributions towards the cost. What can you do to ensure that all children benefit equally when some parents cannot afford the cost? Some heads subsidise the costs for essential visits from their budgets and see them as a legitimate curriculum expense. But this is hardly possible for residential visits of several days. The key to success and to preserve the safety of the children and the staff is sound planning. We suggest you:

- Always follow your LEA guidelines.

- Make sure your Governing Body has a policy which meets the guidelines.

- Inform parents at an early stage of the purpose of the visit, costs, itinerary and insurance arrangements.

- Use approved coach companies and educational centres.

- Develop a comprehensive checklist for the whole staff and make sure that this is followed to the letter.

- Insist that staff make a preliminary visit.

- Be confident in the party leader, that she or he has the necessary skills and experience.

- Double-check all arrangements several days before you go.

- Avoid SATs weeks, parents' evenings, district sports.

Finally, always make sure that you are happy with the arrangements while children and teachers are away. Staff meetings, playground duties and other routines are sometimes overlooked!

EXPENSES

You are entitled to claim for reasonable out-of-pocket expenses. Car journeys in connection with attending meetings and your frantic phone calls to find a supply teacher on a Sunday night are quite legitimate. However, you must always bear in mind that you are using public money. You have to be accountable for every penny: that means keeping scrupulous records, backed up with bills and receipts.

You should consider asking your Governing Body to agree what they consider to be reasonable expenditure. Claim your amounts regularly and make sure that someone else apart from you signs the cheque. Above all, never be tempted to inflate your claims or pass off private expenses for ones in the course of duty. If anyone finds out, it may not just be your maths that is questioned, but your integrity and professional competence to carry on with the job. Open prisons are full of public servants who take just a little more than they are entitled to.

FAILURE

How often do you experience a sense of failure? Every day, frequently, infrequently, occasionally, or never? Do you contribute to the failure of others? Or are you just left to pick up the pieces? Whatever your answers, failure of any kind is an unpleasant experience for whoever is unfortunate enough to be experiencing it!

How do you avoid failure, in yourself and others?
- Set realistic personal targets
- Agree achievable targets for pupils and staff
- Know your limits

- Recognise the limits in others
- Be assertive.

As head you could be prone to feeling a failure because:
- you cannot guard against all financial cuts in expenditure
- you may feel that, in order to achieve the aspirations for your school, you have to "work your staff to the bone"!
- despite all your efforts, you cannot meet the needs of all your pupils
- you seem powerless to protect your pupils against the inequalities of life
- despite your efforts, you are unable to cushion your staff against economic and political constraints.

So you have failed ... Or have you?

Try to keep a sense of perspective in evaluating your own performance and practice, especially any analysis of the contribution of others! If having done all this, you realise that you or others *have* indeed failed, well, remember ... "After all, tomorrow is another day". (*Gone With The Wind*, Margaret Mitchell, 1936.)

FEELINGS

We are all susceptible to feelings and emotions. As head you need to be in control of your feelings as much as you can. The sentiments you feel will vary according to the experience.

You will have feelings of:
- affection
- apprehension
- warmth
- appreciation
- empathy
- concern/compassion
- sympathy
- understanding
- sensitivity
- enjoyment
- happiness.

You may have bad feelings of:
- anger
- dislike
- distrust
- hostility
- hurt.

You will be wise to recognise your wide range of sensations, whether negative or positive. You have been appointed to your post because of the person you are, the person you have become.

You are however, very vulnerable in your role. You must be controlled and considered in all your responses. Over- or under-reaction to a situation will characterize your success as head.

All your reactions need to be measured. Calculate the impact of your counteractions. It is important to conduct yourself with dignity as much as possible. It can, however, be in your interest to display controlled discontent on the rare, but right, occasion. Staff need to be reminded that you too are human! You, too, have feelings! Be cautious, however, never expose yourself to ridicule or lose control.

You must come to terms with the fact that people will only rarely consider your feelings, despite the fact that you give so much of your time and energies to others. Only in exceptional circumstances will gratitude and appreciation be expressed.

"FEMININE" LEADERSHIP
Have you ever pondered on how your sense of gender and sexual identity influences the management of your school?

It could be argued that there has long been confusion in schools about sexual identity and an acceptance of the stereotyping of gender roles. Such imbalances and biases of prejudice will only be laid aside if you are prepared to reflect, with your staff, on the concept of "gender". In so doing, you would do well also to consider gender issues in school management. It may not surprise you to learn that primary heads in the main are:
- collaborative
- creative
- open and tolerant
- experimental
- reflective and intuitive.

Research has found that successful primary school management styles fit a culture perceived by many as "feminine" rather than masculine (Leary, 1985). Secondary heads tend to display characteristics stereotypically considered "masculine". A "feminine" leadership style might be appropriate for your school because "feminine" styles are said to be more accepting of differences than male ones. Question whether or not you are more drawn to your "feminine" or "masculine" side? Are you more at home in administration or management?

Effective heads:
- are intuitive
- take calculated risks
- involve other colleagues
- consider the aesthetics.

...all traditionally "feminine" characteristics!

You may feel more comfortable if the terms masculine and feminine did not predominate so. But remember that we all have distinct personalities without regard to stereotyping... and you might well benefit from pondering on your own sense of gender and sexual identity. Why not consider these influences on your own management style...

FENCES

You encircle your territory... You fence in your pupils and staff! You surround your school with a barricade of some kind.

As head, you must provide a secure environment for your pupils and staff. It is your responsibility to ensure that the uninvited do not make their way in. One way of doing this is to make sure that the school's perimeter fencing remains intact.

How do you do this?
- Build into your caretaker's job description a requirement to keep any perimeter fencing in good repair.
- Remedy any faults as necessary.
- Put into place a rolling programme of repair.

Unavoidable problems:
- gale force winds
- vandalism
- hurricanes
- earthquakes.

All you can do, is your best!

Fences
Question whether or not you are unwilling to commit yourself. Do you sit on the fence? Are you irresolute, uncertain or uncommitted? If you cannot be honest with yourself, question: Is there nobody you can be honest with?

FESTIVALS
Occasions when you celebrate with your pupils, staff, parents, governors and wider community. All festivals should be enjoyable, educational, organised and special. Above all, festivals should be significant and relevant to the work ongoing in school.

Many festivals have a religious origin and you need to be aware of the implications of this. You need to be able to justify the time and effort given to the organisation of any event you sanction in school. Always consider the content and learning aspect of any celebration. What is the aim? If it is just a time of pure enjoyment and revelry, characteristic of our most ancient festivals, be confident to say so.

Despite the fact that we live in an ever-changing, multi-cultural, technological society, many parents will not be happy for their child to participate in a non-Christian festival. Be prepared to cope with bigotry (often from surprising sources). Decide beforehand whether or not your pupils are:
- experiencing
- worshipping
- participating
- acquiring knowledge and understanding.

Empower your staff to encourage the organisation of festivals and events, but remember that 'YOU' are solely accountable. Ensure that the event can be justified and will ultimately benefit the children. If it can, go ahead and make the most of it! Enjoy yourself with your school community!

FIRE DRILL
Fire drills must be conducted regularly in order to prepare pupils and staff for emergency situations.

Regular fire drills must be conducted to ensure that:
- the fire bell is operational
- the building can be evacuated efficiently and effectively
- all in your care have every chance of remaining safe in the case of any emergency.

FIRST AID

It is essential to ensure that all your staff are able to administer first aid competently. Safety must come first but accidents can happen to anyone, at any time, anywhere. Every school has possible danger spots, but with a little forethought you can minimise the risk of accidents.

With this in mind, take a critical tour of your surroundings looking for potential hazards you might not previously have noticed. Do this regularly and in so doing, encourage others to take responsibility too.

Young children are particularly susceptible to accidents. They are naturally inquisitive, unwary and lack the foresight to prevent accidents that an adult could avoid. As it is impossible and indeed undesirable to stop a child exploring the environment, it becomes your responsibility to make your school as safe as possible.

Essential points to remember

You must ensure that your school has a first aid kit and that it is accessible. Items must be replaced as soon as possible and be few and simple. They should be housed in a locked cupboard, preferably wall-mounted and out of reach of children. A portable kit should be available to take on all journeys and for use on sports days and other such events. You must provide opportunities for training for all staff and check that this training is updated. In an emergency you will not have time to consult books, useful as they may be. Seconds will count and speedy action may be vital to save someone's life.

(*See ACCIDENTS; ANTS, WASPS AND BEES.*)

FURTHER STUDY
It might just be your panacea, your elixir, your survival. . . Your

decision to undertake a higher educational course could be for a myriad reasons. But whatever the reason, if you are the student, you and your organisation should benefit in some way. If the potential student is another member of staff, there is no reason why your school should not also benefit. It could in fact be argued that, as head, you have a responsibility to ensure that the whole institution does in fact benefit!

Potential problems if staff are students:
- Funding (who pays... how much)?
- Who benefits?
- Has the student the ability to "give" what the school requires while meeting the demands of the course, and balancing any personal aspirations?
- Can you differentiate between the best needs of your school and the needs of staff? Which come first?
- If the school funds any course, can you expect a return?

While being aware of potential problems, you must also consider the *benefits* of further study. If you are able to manage the situation creatively, your whole school should benefit in addition to the student. Further educational courses are linked to everyday practice in some way or another. Your skill is to expect staff to feed back their learning experiences to the rest of you. Students can be encouraged to "marry" theoretical knowledge with their school practice. The two can be synonymous. Examination and educational research is likely to be worthwhile if the potential problem areas are addressed.

Your school can only develop if those within it are moving forward. In order to advance, you all need to apply yourselves: examine, analyse and research. If you fail to nurture such a thriving ambience, you may unwittingly encourage a climate of complacency and stagnation. You must choose what you would prefer.

GOVERNING BODY

Your Governing Body has, through the various Acts of Parliament since 1988, tremendous power to determine the quality of education you provide. The legal constitution of governing bodies determines that governors will bring a variety of backgrounds, experience and views. But they are partners and stake-holders, they include parents and teachers, and you have to establish a rapport with them in order to achieve your aims as a head.

Work with them. Be open and straightforward in articulating your vision for the development of the school. Tackle the thorny issues of philosophy and finance with openness. Most governing bodies in primary schools are supportive and encouraging and they will normally back you if you are frank. Engage them in the process.

Above all, cultivate a climate of professionalism. Set the highest standards of confidentiality yourself; insist on collective responsibility for the decisions that are taken; recognise that governors need support through training, to take important decisions.

If things go wrong from time to time, accept them as errors rather than attempts to derail your career. All governors are human and the more you encourage them, the greater the support they will give you when you need it.

GRANT-MAINTAINED STATUS
Your Governing Body has to show that it has considered grant-maintained status every year. The Annual Report to Parents has to record this view. Whatever your personal views and those of your governors, the issue must be tackled openly. There are plenty of lobbyists on both sides who will help you prepare a case if you need it.

Above all, keep your personal views to yourself. Once parents or governors know that you have a strong view, it could be used against you. You could find it difficult to make changes in other areas of school life because staff, parents or governors suspect you of ulterior motives.

GROUNDS
School grounds always pose problems for the primary head. They are either too small or too big, and maintenance and security are a constant concern.

But the first thing to remember is that your grounds are part of your school and the children's learning environment. Assert ownership of them by taking your school outdoors. We recommend the following:

- Make your grounds as secure as possible. Careful planting with prickly shrubs is far more effective than barbed wire.
- Encourage the controlled use of your grounds by the local community. Playschemes in the holidays, soccer training after school and cycling awareness courses, will make sure that your grounds are valued by different groups.
- Try to make your grounds functional. Parents will always lend a hand to paint grids and number games on the playground. A few hours on a Saturday morning will work wonders for playground behaviour, giving the children opportunities for constructive play.
- Try to make your grounds attractive. Are there any local sculptors who would like to exhibit their work? How about a mural instead of graffiti on the side of the building?
- Finally, involve the children in decisions about their environment. Enabling them to share in the decision-making also empowers them – to take both ownership and responsibility.

(See also BUILDINGS; FENCES; PONDS.)

HEADTEACHER'S REPORT

It has to be done! The headteacher's termly report to governors . . . an account of the life of the school segmented under such inspirational headings as:

- Organisation and Roll
- Staffing
- Buildings and Maintenance
- Finance
- INSET
- Curriculum
- Visitors
- Events
- Parent/Teacher/Community groups
- Any other commentary

- Confidential items (sometimes!).

There are so many ways in which such a report can be undertaken. The choice is yours! You can write it systematically, weeks in advance (as long as you are prepared to present an out-of-date report at the meeting.). You can write copiously, revealing all and leaving little for the governors to reflect upon. Or you can be as brief as possible, giving the barest of information, just doing your duty as informant to the Governing Body.

There are at least two other options. To write an informative and honest report under great pressure, in the "early hours", just meeting the deadline!.. Or to take the brave decision of committing nothing to paper, in delivering a verbal report. Remember that you do have a choice, as long as you meet the requirements in commenting on all you should.

The headteacher's termly report to governors is what you make it. You are the head. Respond accordingly!

A few other guidelines:
- Always be conscious of the power of the written word.
- Once you have committed yourself to paper you are totally accountable.
- Read and re-read everything you write.
- Be prepared to substantiate the text.
- Be concise, honest and to the point.
- Be aware of libel laws.
- Always include the latest financial computer print-out.
- Celebrate the achievements of your school.
- Be balanced and clear in the points you want to make.

REMEMBER, it's a *report* you are writing, and therefore it should be informative rather than illustrative.

HEALTH

It is very important that you look after your health. You need to experience a sense of well-being if you are to do your job well. In coping with the ever-increasing demands of headship, it is important that you remain fit.

How do you remain healthy?
- Get an adequate amount of sleep.
- Eat sensibly.
- Exercise regularly.
- Allow yourself breaks.
- Recognise when you would benefit from a rest.
- No matter how brief, take a breather.
- Develop the art of relaxation.
- Refresh yourself as appropriate.
- Find yourself a haven.
- Use remedies and dose yourself when necessary.
- Be active.
- Get some fresh air.
- Keep a sense of perspective.

Keeping healthy is about getting to know your body and learning to look after it. If you recognise signs and symptoms of failing health, do something about it as soon as possible. It might just be a matter of taking a well-needed rest, taking a pill or just getting away from it all for a while! If none of these work, go and see your doctor. The correct treatment at the onset of an illness can stop an ailment from getting worse. The recognition of when to take time off could be more cost-effective in the long term. Attempting to struggle on when you need to rest, is not efficient or effective management.

You will more than benefit, and so will your school, if you remind yourself that you are NOT indispensable! If you do not look after yourself and take the odd break, you could unwittingly make yourself dispensable! Think about it. . .
(See DIET; NERVOUS BREAKDOWN; STRESS.)

HEALTH AND SAFETY
LEAs and governing bodies have responsibilities to take all reasonable steps within their power to ensure the health and safety of all those who use school premises. They are required to work together to achieve effective risk control and meet certain standards. Various Acts and Regulations set out the requirements. LEAs will have model health and safety policies for adoption by their schools. Your Governing Body would be

well advised to adopt them formally. You are then assured of LEA legal support in the event of a mishap or legal challenge.

Day-to-day management, and therefore complying with these requirements, is your responsibility. You can minimise the risks by making sure that you have systems in place. The following checklist is a starting point:

- annual recorded check of all electrical equipment
- a job description for your caretaker which specifies weekly inspection of the buildings, paths, carpets, doors, fence
- up-to-date first aid qualifications for key members of staff
- current and accurate lists of contact numbers for all children and staff
- a clear policy for off-site educational visits and residential journeys, adopted by your governors
- annual fire-fighting equipment checks and weekly testing of alarms
- signing-in system for visitors
- licences and insurance for use of premises for out-of-school functions
- record book and Health and Safety proformas to record accidents and near-misses.

If you do have a problem, contact your LEA at once. Seek advice and make sure that your requests and concerns are in writing, preferably copied to your Chair of Governors.
(See ACCIDENTS; DISASTERS; DOGS; FIRE DRILL; FIRST AID; PONDS; PROTECTION; TRESPASSERS.)

HIERARCHY

The hierarchy has long been honoured as a way of getting things done in an organisation. As head you have been given the managerial accountability for your school. You are answerable to the DFE, governors and the LEA for the development of that school.

Managerialism does not have to imply authoritarianism. In exercising the authority vested in your role, you decide the style that suits you and hopefully your school. Authority must be recognised by others, but if as head you do not take into account the feelings of your subordinates, you are most unwise! You too, will suffer in some way.

The roles of head, deputy, teacher and non-teaching staff can be mutually interdependent. You are all reliant to some extent on each other. You therefore need to support each other, in working towards the same ends.

You as head are the only person, in real terms, who is able to cast authoritative judgement over the work of the individual members of your staff. This obviously means that at times such a responsibility can be very demanding. This does mean, however, that you cannot work towards bringing together the various layers of hierarchy in responding to the needs of the school. The hierarchy can provide for the identification and maintenance of corporate accountability. It can also provide for integration.

Your school is about people and your challenge is to nurture and respond to the needs of all your organisational participants. You will find that you need continually to endeavour to form effective relationships, in working positively with all your staff. The beneficiaries will be your pupils, staff, wider community, and YOU!

HOLIDAYS

You are entitled to them, but do you take advantage of your entitlement? If not, why not? What do you gain from going into school during holiday periods? What does the school gain? Is there an expectation that you are in school at certain holiday times; if so, how often do you go in? Do you set yourself impossible work targets during this period? If your answers are, "Yes", you have some problems that need to be looked at!

Holidays are times when you are presented opportunities:
- to rest
- to re-charge
- to do all those jobs you have not had time to do in term
- to read
- to catch up on your backlog of schoolwork
- to reflect
- to do something completely different.

HOMEWORK

There is no reason why you should not do all of these things at different times during the year. If it makes you feel better and will help the new term be easier, then it makes sense to get rid of any backlog of schoolwork. Keep a perspective, however, in doing this. You must have a break, take a rest and do something different. You and your school will gain if you go back after each holiday refreshed. No one will benefit if you do not. Try not to develop a syndrome where you are always using holiday periods to do work that should have been done in term-time. Promise yourself that you will organise your time to keep up with your workload!

You will enjoy your holiday, if you are clear in your expectations of yourself and others.

REWARD YOURSELF WITH A GOOD HOLIDAY. YOU DESERVE IT.

HOMEWORK

You are required to include a statement outlining your homework policy in your school prospectus. Before you can do this you would be wise to negotiate and subsequently discuss an agreed approach with your staff and governors. In so doing, you will undoubtedly arrive at some form of consensus. It is important to have gone through this process as the issue of homework can be a minefield!

Consider:
- reasons for setting homework
- a definition of homework
- what homework you require your pupils to do
- an optimal homework expectation
- the benefits of homework
- negatives
- resourcing
- marking
- parental involvement/pressure.

Policy
If you do not agree a homework policy with your staff you could run into problems. If teachers are regularly giving homework to pupils, question what they are doing with their

pupils during the day. It could be argued that, if children are given a challenging daily programme, they should not be required to do additional work at home. Children are as entitled to leisure time as adults! You and your teachers are the professionals and you need to consider also, how much of your job you want others to do. Will children be psychologically damaged from misguided pressure from other sources? Is there true entitlement for the children who do not receive parental support for their schoolwork?

If you take time to examine the issues raised by homework, you should avoid any resultant problems.

HUMAN RESOURCE MANAGEMENT

Human Resource Management (HRM) is focused on the *people* side of your management. Management is about getting things done. Getting them done through your main resource – people. This is the essence of HRM. It is the *way* you manage your people that is crucial. It is the art of nurturing a sense of satisfaction in each individual and achieving maximum performance from them.

The core functions of general management that embrace HRM are:
- planning
- organisation
- communicating
- evaluating effectiveness.

HRM also has operative functions
- recruitment and selection
- development
- appraisal.

Your function in HRM is to consider:
- your aims
- what you need to develop
- your strategies in order to meet your aims
- how to motivate others in order to achieve your aims.

Your role as manager is critical in HRM. As a successful leader you influence others more than you are influenced by them. You motivate by focusing on the *person* rather than on the *task*.

If you are to manage people effectively, you must develop your communication and negotiation skills well. Central to your leadership and management is the successful establishment of interpersonal relationships.

In motivating your staff, it will be helpful to have a knowledge of the nature of motivation theories. The outcome is so important that you should question whether you can rely solely on your intuition. Allow yourself time to examine educational management research.

A sound and ever-developing theoretical awareness will assist in:
- predicting performance
- job selection
- controlling performance
- achieving desired performance.

You will achieve enhanced performance in yourself and others through a better and more creative management approach. In clarifying and subsequently setting out your own philosophy and approach to Human Resource Management, you and others will benefit.

HUMOUR

A sense of humour is one of the most important assets to possess in headship.

The ability to appreciate and express oneself in humorous situations is invaluable. The capability to create jocularity from ordinary situations is to your advantage.

You spend a significant percentage of your time at school. In this environment you will be constantly challenged. You will survive if you can manipulate each situation. If you acquire the capacity to accommodate a variety of behavioural traits by responding pleasantly, you will survive.

Having the confidence to jest, and recognising when to flatter and indulge, is part of your professional maturity in headship. Life can be a serious experience. But it can also be an enjoyable one. Rather than dwell on the areas over which we have no control, try to identify the humour within. Why not exploit it to advantage?

As head, you want all your staff and children to be happy. In order to cultivate a sense of fun:

- nurture humour
- exploit good times
- be light-hearted
- be alert.

Never:
- poke fun
- ridicule
- send up.

You have integrity: make sure that this is apparent at all times. Enjoy the company of your pupils and staff. Above all, have good, honest-to-goodness FUN.

ILLNESS

Unlike other professions, we cannot regulate the input and output of our work. Paperwork, orders and production rates in other jobs can be adjusted according to the level of resources available. But in teaching, the raw material we work with – the children – are always there, bright and eager to learn. You don't have the option of asking parents to keep their children at home. Somehow, the primary head has to maintain security for the children and continuity of their curriculum.

So illness of staff can present major problems. The cost of buying in supply cover can make a huge hole in the budget. And if you try to cover for an absent colleague yourself or by splitting a class, you risk generating extra stress and pressure.

Most heads have a strategy for the occasional one- or two-day absence. You might elect to provide cover yourself for the first day and then buy-in a supply, or use a part-time support teacher if you are lucky enough to have one. Whatever plan you use should be clear to everyone. Your LEA may step in and fund cover after a certain period. You need to check. Try to solve the problems before they start.

(See HEALTH; NERVOUS BREAKDOWN.)

INDUSTRIAL DISPUTES

Industrial action and schools don't mix. The inevitable charge that children are being used as political pawns will inflame passions and obscure the issues. The primary head is in a very difficult position with loyalties to different groups – teachers, parents, governors – and pupils. Groups and individuals will oppose each other and because you are the most powerful person in the organisation, everyone will want you on their side.

Unless of course you are yourself a participant, the best advice must be to keep a safe distance from the action and avoid being drawn into taking a stance which will be used against you. Your job is to keep calm when everyone else is creating mayhem and to manage a difficult period with the childrens' interests uppermost in your mind. If you keep a cool head and avoid being judgemental or recriminatory, the sooner you will be able to get back to normal and repair relationships when the dust has settled. You will also survive with your integrity intact. And you need that to continue to lead.

Nationally, teachers are a conservative profession and there is still a strong feeling of vocation. Many will give their last ounce of energy for their pupils. On the other hand, as well as being a profession, teaching is also a job. In certain circumstances, teachers may feel that they need to exercise their rights as any other employees.

In the case of a dispute, we recommend you seek advice from:
- your professional association
- your LEA
- any other relevant bodies.

You can also seek information from teachers' unions. Do remember, however, that prevention is better than cure. So avoid disputes if you can.

INITIAL TEACHER TRAINING

The choice of routes for students to train as teachers is varied. As head you cannot assume that all students, or newly qualified teachers are getting or have received, a similar experience. Here is an outline of current training methods to help you avoid problems that could arise through a lack of understanding of what they involve:

Initial Education Programmes:
- 4-year full-time Bachelor of Education (B.Ed.)
- 3-year full-time six subject B.Ed.
- 1-year full-time Post Graduate Certificate in Education (P.G.C.E.)
- 2-year shortened B.Ed., (mainly for students with technical and business qualifications)
- 2-year part-time P.G.C.E.
- Articled and Licensed Teacher Schemes

Range of students on such courses:
- mixture of ages
- diverse backgrounds
- diverse education experiences
- diverse educational qualifications

You may question the diversity of such programmes, but there is a reason for it. The range of entrants is such that no one programme could provide an adequate course. Also, teaching itself is such a complex and varied activity that the profession requires a wide range of different qualities. People will decide to become teachers for different reasons and at different ages.

The demands placed on teachers have changed with time. This has led to the development of new programmes of study. The main aim for schools and training establishments should be the production of a high quality of teaching, which depends on more than mere training. Quality teaching skills can only be learned via a positive approach from student, schools and tutors. *(See MENTORS).*

IN-SERVICE TRAINING (Inset)
All those who work in schools have an entitlement to ongoing professional development. Our human resources are our most costly investment and they need looking after to make sure that they have the skills to do the jobs we want them to.

The problems which arise are usually to do with poor planning or inappropriate, or inadequate, training. You can make your in-service training programme effective and avoid problems by following a few simple guidelines:

- Plan your training needs well in advance, as part of your overall School Development Plan.

- Match your budget distribution for training against your curriculum development priorities.

- Make sure that your governors and staff have been involved in identifying priorities.

- Consult staff about their individual training needs as part of your professional development discussions. Make sure that a proportion of the budget is allocated to meeting these.

- Retain some of your budget for courses and initiatives at short notice.

- Always evaluate the outcomes of in-service training.

INTERVENTION

Making a decision, as head, concerning intervention can be problematic. You want to empower others by allowing tasks to be developed to a successful conclusion, and yet you may be tempted to intervene in a situation for a variety of reasons.

You are challenged to intervene when:
- the level of noise in a class appears to have reached a level that you find unacceptable
- you witness unacceptable behaviour
- you overhear parent/staff discussions with which you feel uncomfortable
- children break school rules whilst in the care of parents
- staff give incorrect information to pupils/parents
- members of staff shout unnecessarily or loudly at children or each other
- you become aware of pupils being harshly, inappropriately or unnecessarily punished;
- students are seen, or seem, to be mis-managing situations.

In order for any *intervention* not to be interpreted as *interference*, you need to contemplate your actions carefully.

Ask yourself, whether you :
- are jumping to conclusions
- have made your expectations clear
- have a right to intervene
- will damage relationships
- are being dictatorial
- can help the situation
- need to observe the situation
- need to evaluate and consider your actions
- would be more effective in taking alternative actions later.

If, having considered all these issues, you *still* feel that your pupils or school are at risk, or will be damaged in some way, your intervention is justified. No matter how offended others will be by your intervention, you must always put the needs of your pupils and school first!

You can intervene in such a way that the other person/s will not lose their dignity. Always follow up any intervention by explaining why you found the situation unacceptable. This will hopefully prevent it happening again.

INTERVIEWS

Interviews for staff appointments have enormous potential to go wrong. In teaching, candidates tend to be interviewed on the same day and the decision declared at the end of the proceedings. It doesn't have to be so. But it usually happens that way because of the time constraints and the need to convene governors to form a panel.

Most problems arise through lack of planning. Check the following, so that the candidates and the interviewers get the best out of the process:

● Be generous in the time you allow for the whole day. Build in breaks for comfort, tea and walks around the building, for interviewers and candidates.

● Make sure that the candidates know when they will be interviewed and by whom. Do they need to be on the premises all the time? Can they leave as soon as they have been interviewed? When will the final decision be made known?

- Assign a comfortable area for the candidates and detail someone to look after them. Provide refreshments and have some flowers and magazines. Introduce them to each other and those involved in the process. Show them where the toilets are and where they can make a phone call. If there are more than a few, name-badges are a good idea.

- Choose your interview room with care. A room at the hub of your school may be fine for you as head but too noisy for interviewing candidates. Arrange your furniture with care. Avoid desks at all costs. Leave space between the chairs and make sure they are not of different sizes. Provide a jug of water for the tongue-tied. Agree in advance who will collect the candidates and make the introductions.

- Stick to the order and the questions that you have agreed.

- When the decision is made and the successful candidate has accepted, thank all the candidates personally and arrange to de-brief them.

Finally, don't forget to thank all those who made the day a success, and discuss with them how it might be improved next time round.

JARGON

Jargon can be your lingo, the educational patois that enables you to communicate with a select few: those who (pretend to) understand the essence of your common "speak"! You may feel that jargon may well be your saving-grace, but it could equally be an irritant to those who are not party to your idiom, tongue, or balderdash! Remember that the use of jargon is exclusive and, as such, it alienates those who do not speak in your prescribed code.

A positive view of Jargon:
- an agreed code only understood by those whom you want to understand, those with whom you want to be in tune;
- an economical use of language;
- a challenging interpretation of educational terminology.

A negative view of jargon:
- you need to keep up with the frequency of change in lingo;
- others feel left out;
- its usage could be seen as elitist;
- you could be seen to be running away from everyday accepted language norms;
- you need to question why you feel more secure in using jargon.

Just think about what you are endeavouring to say.

What are the messages you want to convey?

Whatever your answer, choose the most effective means of communication: the one to suit you and to include others.

JOB SPECIFICATIONS

A job description gives details, normally in writing, of a post which has a place in the whole staffing establishment aimed at satisfying demands upon the school. It is used to fit the postholder into the staff team and it is made available to candidates for the post when it falls vacant. It should stipulate the main requirements of the post and school expectations of the holder or would-be holder. Any specification should complement the agreed role criteria.

In making job specifications available, problems can arise if you:
- do not consult your governors
- cannot agree with your governors
- are too specific
- attempt to rewrite or supplement contracted duties
- are too vague
- are not consistent in your expectations throughout the whole process
- fail to discuss changes with existing postholders.

Be cautious in committing requirements to paper, as you can be called to account for anything you put in writing. You can be challenged for undelivered promises, raised expectations or inaccurate information. The job specification is likely to be a prospective candidate's initial link with your school. It will inevitably make an impression and you desire this to be a favourable one.

Potential problems will be avoided if you:
- involve your governors in all stages of the selection process
- allow sufficient time to agree selection criteria
- agree a job specification based on stated criteria
- consider contractual obligations
- consider financial implications
- observe terms of equal opportunities
- use simple direct language.

In creating a good impression of your school you would do well to think carefully about presentation. In so doing, consider the quality of paper, type-font, grammar and spelling. Question whether the content is inviting.

Ask yourself: in different circumstances would you be interested in the post if presented with this proposed job specification?

JUDGEMENT

To judge too quickly could be your downfall or that of someone-else! Try to be prudent before passing judgement on anything or anyone! Endeavour to diagnose the situation, to examine and evaluate before even attempting any form of judgement.

Why? Because judgement of any kind can:
- determine one's views and those of others
- sentence
- convict, constrict and constrain
- encourage value judgements
- punish
- discriminate.

In developing an ability to judge, you:
- make critical judgements
- achieve a balanced viewpoint.

KINDNESS

To express kindness is to be amiable, compassionate, tolerant and humane. These are all worthy leadership qualities and ones that you, as head, would do well to express in your role.

A few kind words, said at the right time, can make all the difference to your children, staff, parents and governors. If you have transmitted your philosophy and ethos successfully, you should be able to identify and develop a rapport with a significant number of the stake-holders in your school.

It goes without saying that the relationship with the children in your school should be an example to all. It will be so, if it is based on tolerance, respect and kindness. If you endeavour to empathise with children and adults, it will be easier to be kind!

In exercising kindness yourself, do not neglect to recognise it in others. Encourage and favour kindliness. Conversely, do not become complacent if there is a lack of goodness and understanding within your school. Habits of kindness in children and staff can only enhance the school philosophy and ethos.

LATENESS

How do you deal with the unpunctual, those who arrive at the last minute? It's a particular problem for you if it happens to be a member of staff. It means that the person is unprepared to start the day. A colleague's lateness has a negative affect on the morale of all staff, whether directly affected or not.

What do you do?
- Keep a log of arrival times.
- Catalogue the effect on practice.
- Re-visit the job specification and job description.
- Check when the person in question is leaving.

When you are certain of your facts, confront! Keep calm and discuss the implications of the problem. Refer to your log, job specification and job description as appropriate. You specify the times, so do not allow yourself to be side-tracked if hours are being made up elsewhere. Try to find out why lateness is occurring; there might be domestic or health problems that you can discuss and hopefully help with. Keep a distanced-eye on the revised pattern. Lateness is not easily solved. You will have to act again if punctuality is not maintained, so keep any documentation.

How do you cope with those who are late for appointments with you?

This can be a constant irritation. Your day's plan is upset by those turning up late. It is difficult to get on with anything substantial while waiting as the person/s might well come at any time. While you are waiting, you could:
- get on with those simple tasks you have been meaning to do for some time
- read.

When the appointee arrives:
- see them but only for what is left of your planned time;
- be polite but make it clear that you have other commitments;
- If they turn up after the allotted time, make another appointment unless you feel it is more important to go ahead with the meeting than do other things.

If YOU are the late-comer evaluate why. Are you:
- not planning your time well
- taking-on too much
- too readily available?

Whatever the reason, you must do something about it! If you are late it will have a detrimental affect on the whole organisation. *(See ABSENCES.)*

LEADERSHIP
Situations continually arise that necessitate appropriate action to be taken for their resolution. It could be argued that this can only be done by those best suited to deal with the ensuing problem. This could be irrespective of hierarchical position or status.

As head you have the overall responsibility for your organisation. That does not mean, however, that all authority must emanate from you. Do not expect or even allow all initiatives to be confined to you as an individual and as head. Encourage sharing and empower others to realise their potential.

You are the leader.

If you are truly confident and competent in your leadership skills and management qualities, you will feel enabled, and secure, when you allow "sharing" to take place. Others can only be involved in decision-making if you invite them to do so. As head, you are a consultant and a researcher. As such, you look for ways in which all adult members of your school can honestly and positively regard each other. You find ways that facilitate shared responsibility for their, and your, organisation.

As an effective leader, do you:
- empower others
- put the needs of others first
- allow others to take the lead
- know when you must lead
- recognise the distinction between leadership and management?

Ask yourself whether or not you can put the needs of your organisation before your own. If you can, then you have the potential to become an effective and successful leader! And others will feel secure in your leadership.
(See FEMININE LEADERSHIP, MANAGEMENT.)

LETTINGS

You are only too aware that you are expected to generate income for your school! One way to do this, is to hire out your school building. There are many groups who are willing to hire the premises for which you are responsible. But despite the bucks rolling in, there are pitfalls:

- a cavalier attitude to the premises
- essential school resources damaged or "missing"
- teachers complaining about the state of their teaching area
- an invasion of privacy
- a total lack of comprehension of what you stand for
- petty vandalism and damage to property.

When you spend the afternoon before each letting preparing as if for an air-raid, and the morning after each letting placating teachers and organising the clearing-up brigade, you seriously consider whether it's worth the effort! Are you losing more than you are gaining?

What is the answer?
- Draw up a code of conduct for all hirers.
- Get the hirers to agree by signing the code/contract.
- Meet the hirers at semi-regular intervals to discuss how things are going.
- Make your hirers welcome but nurture a respect for your premises.
- Make staff aware that you are prepared to "work at it".
- Show by example, in always leaving the school "as you would wish to find it".
- Encourage your hirers to do the same.
- Be assertive, recognise when you do have "to pull the plug".

(See BUILDINGS.)

LISTS
Lists can be the bane of your life or lists can be your saving grace.

You itemise your proposed use of time. You record names, appointments and things to do. You print-out your day, evening, week, and section-out your time. You prioritise your tasks, neatly written one under the other.

In cataloguing your time you are directing your attention, and often that of others, to your successes and failures. Often the inventory is displayed and highlighted for all to see. Consciously or unconsciously, you desire others to be aware of all you have to do. If your register is crossed-through or ticked, you feel justifiably proud of your achievements. If, however, your list remains untouched or has only one or two favourable markings, you experience a sense of failure.

You need to consider:
- the benefits of list-making
- the time spent in recording
- whether or not lists are helpful to you
- the effect on others.

Ask yourself whether or not you need an additional written

schedule of your time. Could you respond as well by referring to a well-kept diary and up-to-date calendar? The time spent in carefully tabulating your day might well be better used in actually tackling and completing your tasks! Seriously evaluate the wisdom of list-making.

Invoicing your commitments may well be the spur for you to complete each one! If you know this to be the case, carry on with your personal time syllabus. If, however, you spend precious time indexing your day and then either ignore the list – or make another one – you have a problem! One that can hopefully be solved.

Put the CONSIDERATION aside.

Get on with the DOING.

Enjoy the ACTION . . .

LOCAL MANAGEMENT OF SCHOOLS
One of the main changes of the Education Reform Act (1988) was a greater delegation to schools of the responsibility for financial and other aspects of management.

You as head are responsible for the good and whole management of your school. The underlying principles of such management means that you have to account for the funds of your school. You are required to exercise managerial and financial responsibilities. You must use public funds to advantage in:
- giving value for money
- administrating
- managing
- planning and budgeting
- controlling finances
- using management information to advantage.

Local Management of Schools has increased the workload of the head. As well as being an occasional teacher, you also need to administer finances efficiently and effectively. You need accounting abilities. You are totally accountable for the financial management of your school!

What do you do?

- Plan strategically.
- Monitor operations and feedback.
- Amend and update plans.
- Report on performance.
- Detail development plans, including budgets.
- Keep your governors fully informed.
- Be in control, but be accountable to all.

Local management has given heads freedom. If you have the funds, you can use funds effectively, efficiently and creatively. If you have not, you are constrained and limited in what you can offer your pupils and their parents. You will appear to be the one responsible for difficult decisions, made through the lack of finance. Local Management of Schools has made it incumbent on schools to "get bums on seats". You, as head, must manage finances well on behalf of your governing body.

You must survive, and in so doing, keep your head! It's just another aspect of your role, which you can manage if you keep it in perspective. (*See also BUSINESS*.)

MANAGEMENT

Management is a form of control and also, hopefully, support and facilitation.

As a manager you:
- administrate
- direct
- care
- govern
- conduct
- control
- operate
- supervise
- guide.

As a manager you need to consider whether you are reactive or pro-active. There will be some events that you cannot anticipate and therefore you can only react, as you feel appropriate. If, however, you have a vision that has been shared and translated into a long-term plan, you can be proactive. Staff will know what is expected of them and together you will endeavour to make the theory become practice within your school.

As head, you exercise different managerial skills and behaviours as the situation demands. You can work alongside your colleagues encouraging collective decision-making and nurturing a shared responsibility for the school's development. You cannot decide what others do, but you can help each to respond to problems as their skills and dispositions allow. In working thus, with your colleagues, you are cultivating a sense of continuous collegiality. As an effective manager you respect your staff and, in so doing, empower them.

Do not expect staff to always be:
- amenable
- compliant
- docile
- governable
- tractable.

There will be times when you seem to manage with ease, but all too often the process can be demanding and challenging. It is worth remembering that your school exists for its members and for their happiness. Do not reject or resent the "angst" of organisational life. Why not welcome it as healthy and exciting! It can be, and by working through it, you will experience a sense of achievement and happiness. *(See also BUSINESS.)*

MARKETING

Marketing is an emotive subject. Many heads feel it is alien to educational culture. But without strategies for promoting or marketing your school, you will be in the slow lane when it comes to keeping your numbers – and your budget – healthy. Without a healthy roll, the problems will come thick and fast: redundancies, curriculum spending reductions, vertical grouping will all follow. Everyone wants to be associated with success – and that goes for children, teachers and parents. So it's worth spending a little time working out your plans.

Marketing need not be aggressive. All you need to do is to make sure that you keep your market share and don't lose pupils to your competitors. That doesn't mean that you have to compete. The following may help focus your ideas.

- Have your governors set up a Publicity and Marketing group.

- Look at the presentation of all your written material. Get rid of Banda machines and worn-out copiers. Invest in some stylish headed notepaper. Make your brochure as glossy and inviting as possible. Use your school colours and logo on everything.

- Spend some money on creating areas on public view as attractive as possible. Tubs, shrubs and direction signs make visitors feel welcomed.

- Be quite clear about how you want the phones answered and people received. Is there an attractive area for parents and visitors to wait when they have an appointment with you? Do you stick to time?

- Get someone else to look at your office and give an honest opinion. Is it a reject from the filmset of the Munsters with utility furniture laden with yellowing files? If so, you may be losing more parents than you think.

MEDIA

The local and national media will be interested in any story which catapaults your school into the limelight. It could be your Ofsted report, or the achievement of a pupil or member of staff. If the attention is welcome and celebrates something your school can be proud of, a simple prepared sound-byte from you will enhance the status of your school and buy you free publicity.

But what do you do if the story is malicious or untrue? Disaffected parents or governors may well contact the press. Issues such as provision for special needs, the style of a particular teacher, playground bullying, staffing levels or competitive sports are considered fair game.

Unwanted media attention has to be managed with kid gloves. The golden rule is to say nothing which you have not prepared. If the matter is subject to legal proceedings, say that you have no comment. You could end up in deep water if you comment on something that is *sub judice*. Clear what you say with your LEA or governors first. Don't be rail-roaded into taking calls from reporters on the hop. If reporters or TV crews arrive, be polite, but refuse to talk until you have agreed what you will say with your LEA or Governing Body. Have phone calls screened and say you will call back. Most LEAs have a press officer whom

MEETINGS

As a primary head, you could spend most of your life in meetings. Governors, cluster groups, parents, curriculum, educational psychologists all demand your time and can become a problem. You need to determine how many of them are necessary, and how many actually need *you* to be there.

Try to get into the habit of the "good meeting" test. Before you arrange a meeting or attend one, spare a few minutes on the following.

- What is the purpose of the meeting? Who is the chair? Who is responsible for minute/note taking? Do you expect decisions to be made?

- Are you fully briefed on the content? Have you all the background information, including minutes from the previous meetings? Have you done the things you said you'd do? Do you have an agenda?

- How long will the meeting be? Can you afford to spend the whole time there? Or could you attend just for certain agenda items? Have you included time travelling to and from the meeting?

- Make sure you arrive on time and leave when the meeting is due to finish. People will value your time if you do.

- If you are responsible for action following the meeting, try to get it done on the day. Build in some time *immediately afterwards* for writing up minutes and checking the agenda for the next meeting. Minutes received within a day or two after a meeting have greater value. Those present will have a clearer recollection of the business covered.

Finally, if you are over-run with pressures, don't think twice about sending a properly briefed delegate. Primary heads never know what may happen with children or staff from day to day. Sometimes, you just have to clear your diary to cope with a crisis. It's better to phone your apologies in good time than arrive late and unprepared. And sitting in a meeting when your mind is on something else is a waste of everyone's time.

MENSTRUATION

One in ten girls start their periods while still at primary school, a painful and often embarrassing complication to their school day. Problems can be eased by ensuring that:

- the locks work on the lavatory doors (or the girls have access to a more private W.C.)

- a female member of staff is available to help with comfort, advice and supplies.

- the children know who this is (and trust her).

In recognising the important part that your school can play in preparing girls for menstruation, you will hopefully deal with the consequences practically and sensitively. Everyone will then benefit.

MENTORING

Mentoring can be a structured or non-structured transferable transaction between two people for a specific set of reasons. A mentor can be seen as a guide who supports a protegé during an induction period. A mentee can be a newly-qualified teacher, student in practice, or head in their first year in post.

Problems that can arise in mentoring tend to be linked to:
- selection
- time allocation
- status
- hierarchical structures
- influence
- value systems
- dependency
- relationships
- responsibilities.

Before you agree to enter into a mentoring programme, seriously consider the implications for your school. Think about the capabilities of your teachers and their responsibilities to their pupils. Teacher mentors should be primarily concerned with the needs of the pupils within their care. The needs of the mentee must always come second to these and it can be difficult for some practitioners to balance the responsibilities of both roles.

The mentee will benefit if the mentor has the qualities of:
- calmness
- deliberation
- patience
- mediation.

And has developed skills as a:
- listener
- communicator
- observer
- consultant.

You need to be confident that your would-be mentor has analysed the reasons for taking on the role. A mentor needs energy, time and commitment and needs to be secure in themselves as a person!

You will benefit as a school if you involve all staff in the process to some extent. If a mutually supportive structure is nurtured, time can be negotiated to cover for observation, evaluation, and meetings with the partner institution.

If you are or desire to be a mentor head, the considerations are similar. Whatever type of mentoring you embark upon, a policy should be put into place regarding the entitlements and expectations of all parties. Remember that you are entering into a formal contract and, as such, have obligations.
(See STUDENTS.)

MIDDAY SUPERVISION

Dealing with problems over the lunchtime break can occupy a great deal of time. You have legal responsibility and it is up to you to organise adequate supervision and routines. You can minimise problems in the following ways.

● Establish and fill a sufficient number of supervisor posts to cope with the numbers of children who stay.

● Provide training and clear instructions for the management of children. Some LEAs run courses and there are video training packages on the market.

- Have regular meetings with your team of supervisors.

- Try to develop a sense of partnership between your teachers and the supervisors. Allocate supervisors to particular year groups or classes.

- Invite supervisors to share in the children's work through accompanying day visits. Encourage them to help run lunchtime clubs. This helps to develop relationships.

- Involve supervisors in decisions about creative play and games activities. You may have a supervisor who enjoys chess or macramé. Make use of their talents.

- Have your playground area marked with grids, hopscotch, number snakes, maps, circles, chess-boards, roadways and other features which will interest and involve the children.

- Invest some money in small play equipment and make this the responsibility of your supervisors. Skipping ropes, plastic balls, outdoor chess and other items are quite cheap.

- Consider using indoor areas for certain activities. Some children are far happier sitting and reading or drawing than charging about on a boisterous playground.

NATIONAL CURRICULUM

The 1988 Education Reform Act requires all maintained schools to provide for all pupils, within the compulsory years of schooling, a basic curriculum. This is known as the National Curriculum. From 1988, all children became entitled to a broad, balanced and differentiated curriculum. This must also promote the moral, spiritual, cultural, mental and physical development of pupils in preparing them for the wider experiences of adult life.

As head, you must ensure that all your pupils have full entitlement and have access to equality of opportunity.

Few would argue that the main aim of the Act was to make schools more accountable. Testing and assessment at 7, 11, 14 and 16 are integral to the National Curriculum. A testing process such as this can be seen as true public accountability. You may well question whether it is the teachers or the pupils who are the object of scrutiny.

So how do you exercise your responsibilities in ensuring that the National Curriculum is a reality in your school?

- Promote the positives for the children
- Encourage co-operative planning.
- Build in monitoring systems.
- Celebrate the achievement of your children and staff.
- Observe your statutory duties.
- Be realistic in your expectations.
- Consider workload in suggesting additional school activities.
- Fine-tune the National Curriculum to complement your own school's ethos and philosophy.
- Streamline.
- Involve all staff in developing simple systems.
- Utilise the strengths of all staff.
- Develop a challenging and stimulating curriculum, as well as a broad, balanced and differentiated one.
- Keep your finger on the curriculum pulse.

After the introduction of the National Curriculum, things seem to have reached a form of equilibrium. . . or did, before the Dearing Report. (1993). But that's another discussion *(See DEARING.)*

NEGATIVISM

Negativism can present problems if you allow it to infiltrate your organisation. This can happen surreptitiously and will permeate the fabric of your school.

In order to deal with any negativism, you need to be constantly aware of those who exhibit tendencies to be negatively critical. Beware, and aware of the sceptics and those who make derisive comments.

What can you do? You can counter negativism with RESISTANCE! In being constantly aware, you:

- challenge
- confront
- undermine
- subvert.

In countering negativism with positivism, you work consistently at:

- affirming good practice
- congratulating and rewarding
- being assertive
- being decisive
- being constructive
- encouraging all to be appropriately expressive.

In so doing, the staff will be forward-thinking, effective, and supportive of each other. You will be practical, productive and as a consequence progressive. It only takes one negative colleague, parent or governor to sow the seeds of discontent! In promoting the best for your school and those within it, you need to contradict contrary behaviour.

In developing strategies to cope with any negativism:
- encourage people to come to you to express their feeling
- listen and genuinely consider their viewpoint
- have a supportive network of informants
- plan any response
- use your position, in taking advantage of available opportunities
- be fair, balanced and equitable.

In recognising negativism in your school, question your own demeanour. If you are negative, you will breed negative traits in others. You will de-stabilize and develop insecurity throughout the whole school. If you do not like coming to school and do not respond positively to the current educational climate, why should others?

NEGOTIABLES

In exercising your management style there will be some areas of your developing practice that you will be prepared to negotiate on, and others that you will ensure remain sacrosanct. If you, and others, are clear about your philosophy, you will have no difficulty in making the necessary definitions.

Whether or not you promote a collegial approach or have a more directive style of management, you will need to bargain, mediate and conciliate with staff, parents, governors and, at times, other colleagues.

As a successful head, you need to reflect carefully before you enter into any form of arbitration. You would do well to consider what you believe to be unnegotiable and why! It is likely that there will be few non-negotiables but any will be very important to you. Essentially, your ideals and principles are within this protected zone.

Non-negotiables:
- values
- principles
- ethics
- ideology.

Every person with whom you interact will feel more secure in the knowledge that you show determination in protecting your basic beliefs. You will also gain well-earned respect if you display flexibility and are genuine in involving others in relevant decision-making.

In achieving consensus, you will exercise the skills of:
- ambassador
- mediator
- moderator
- delegator.

You will NEGOTIATE. In so doing you will favourably involve and empower others. In return you will be rewarded by their support, commitment and loyalty. Together you will enjoy the benefit of developing a successful team: a successful school.

NEGOTIATION

In order to achieve your objectives, you will employ negotiation skills. You will learn to arbitrate, conciliate, mediate and transact in your internal and external communications. Negotiation skills do not come naturally to many.

In negotiation, plan and prepare:
- your best position
- your worst negotiated alternative
- your limit

- a framework
- predict and forecast the other party's case
- prepare your own case
- decide on the style you will portray.

In negotiation, be open:
- in stating what you want
- in requesting feedback
- in listening to what the other party wants
- in giving feedback.

In negotiation, test and bargain:
- state positional differences
- explore options.

In negotiation, follow up:
- in recording understanding
- checking understanding
- confirming that the relationship is intact.

NERVOUS BREAKDOWN

"Here comes your nineteenth nervous breakdown." (Rolling Stones, 1964; Womacx B & S Kags Music.)

A nervous breakdown is when a person collapses or breaks down through psychiatric illness. This is often characterised by irritability, depression or tiredness. In your time as head you will observe signs of nervous disorder in your colleagues. You may even recognise such agitation within yourself.

How do you recognise the signs?
- extreme tiredness
- irritability
- depression
- nonspecific or ill-defined physical complaints
- a feeling of not being in control
- a feeling of an inability to cope
- over/under-reaction.

What can you do?

To help others, you need to be sympathetic but not over-indulgent. Try to assist in the recognition of the problem. Never, however, allow your pupils to suffer! No matter how "cruel" you feel you have to be, remember that the welfare of your pupils must always come first. If at any time you feel they are at risk, you must take assertive action. Support as necessary but insist on a "rest" if appropriate.

If *you* are the one who needs help, go out and get it! A day or two in bed at the right time might well be the remedy. If not, then seek advice, insist on some space and time to yourself. Time to restore and to revitalise!

The nervous system is just another part of your bodily processes. You have not failed, or lost all, if you feel that you need to take time out. Professional maturity is about knowing when to take action. Only you know if you just need a "breather", or need "to get out" altogether. Never make the latter decision without due consideration. Evaluate carefully before resolving any problem in this way.

Your thought processes are "well challenged" in headship. Do not be unduly surprised, therefore, if they demand an occasional rest. *(See HEALTH.)*

NEWCOMERS
New arrivals to your school come in all guises:
- reception entrants
- other entrants
- newly qualified teachers
- new members of staff.

All newcomers will experience the emotions of an outsider. They have recently arrived and will be starting to participate in the every day life of your school. To them, all routines will seem strange and even alien. They may feel disinclined to engage in the infrastructure of the school. As new members of staff, they will be wary of engaging in staff-room conversation and will be uncertain of general school routines. New children will often feel lonely and confused. As head, you have a responsibility to assist all newcomers. You have a duty to initiate and develop relationships with children and staff. You have obligations to make things easier for all concerned.

How do you help?
- be welcoming

- take time to explain procedures
- have a Staff Handbook
- discuss, and agree, general school processes with all staff
- ask someone to take a special interest in each newcomer
- monitor the development of each novice – child or adult
- nurture in your newcomer an appreciation and understanding of the philosophy and ethos of your school.

The ability to empathise with the feelings of all newcomers is essential. Whether to a pupil or a teacher, the time given to an induction process will be more than worthwhile.

Time spent in welcoming and introducing new children, parents and staff to help them gain an understanding of the framework of your organisation will be rewarded.

Your school will benefit if all its contributors and participants are happy, secure and fulfilled.

In achieving this, you too will prosper.

NEWLY QUALIFIED TEACHERS

Newly qualified teachers are teachers who are in their first year of teaching. Despite the fact that the job of teaching can be viewed as hazardous, many continue to train as teachers. They enter the profession through a variety of routes and therefore bring differing experiences with them.

Although officially there is no longer a probationary year, you could consider the first year as having the induction features of probation. All new entrants deserve support if they are to be given the chance to do justice to the children, themselves and to your school.

Your newly qualified teacher will become a good practitioner by:

- having the opportunity to plan co-operatively
- being part of a team
- being given time to reflect, amend and develop
- having the support of a teacher mentor
- having the support of all colleagues
- having the support of you, as head
- being accountable
- being given regular feedback in planned time

- being given opportunities for Inset
- being given opportunities to observe good practice
- being given opportunities to work alongside other practitioners
- being welcomed and valued
- being given constructive criticism.

You will reap the benefits if you plan a balanced support programme for your NQT. If you build in a requirement for written lesson preparation and evaluation, with regular feedback sessions, you will nurture theoretical and practical development. As well as empowering your teacher mentor, do allow yourself a monitoring role too. It will be well worth the effort and time involved.

Be constructive, supportive and honest at all times and you will gain the respect of your newly qualified teacher. It won't do you any harm to consider when you were at the early stages of your career. What would you have benefited from? Remember . . .
(See INITIAL TEACHER TRAINING, MENTORS, PROBATIONARY PERIOD.)

NON-TEACHING STAFF
Problems are more likely to arise with non-teaching staff if you have divisions within your staffing structure. You need to question whether or not, consciously or unconsciously, you create staffing boundaries.

Question:
- who uses the staff room
- who receives information concerning whole school development
- stages of received information
- whether all staff have a job description
- whether all staff are subject to an appraisal system
- whether all staff are fully aware of the philosophy, ethos and aims of the school
- whether all staff take a measure of responsibility for the behaviour of your pupils.

If you feel that all staff are equal but with different roles to play within your organisation, you need to apply yourself in making this a reality. Everyone in your school needs to know what is expected of them. This means that you need to give quality time to all your staff in nurturing shared aims and making the school ethos and philosophy a reality.

How can you be all things to all persons?
- be realistic
- have regular meetings with all staff
- consider the occasional whole-school staff meeting held at a time to suit everyone
- make explicit your ethos, philosophy, aims and behaviourial aspirations.

As head, you will challenge inappropriate work practice from any member of staff. In developing an effective and successful school, you do not confine this to teachers only. Everyone must work positively together in order to meet the needs of your school and to provide the very best for the children within it.

OPEN ENROLMENT
Under the Education Reform Act of 1988, you have to accept all children until your standard number is reached. Your Governing Body will be asked by the LEA to agree the standard number annually. This can cause serious problems. You cannot refuse to accept a child, even if your class sizes are high in that particular year group. If your Governing Body has agreed an optimum ceiling figure for class size, you will have to gain agreement to breach that figure or to re-organise your classes. Vertical grouping or additional teaching resources may be the answer. But mid-year this may prove disruptive.

Open enrolment encourages parents to be consumers in the education market place. It also encourages schools to compete with each other for pupils. Schools are now quite used to presenting their philosophy and practice but many heads still find it difficult to adopt a competitive approach, where neighbouring schools will be winners or losers. Most heads are content to have on roll those children from within their reserved area and not actively poach children from outside. However, there are examples of heads who leaflet neighbouring areas or place advertisements in their local papers.

The problems are that you either have too few pupils and therefore lack the budget to sustain the quality and range of educational opportunity to which your school aspires. Alternatively, your school may be over-subscribed and may not have the capacity to cope with an influx of out-of-area children.

The professional and dignified middle path for state school heads is to ensure that you are not gaining children at the expense of other local schools. But in some areas, private or grant-maintained schools may have the advantage of better resourcing. You may also be competing against state schools which have nursery provision, on-site playgroups or community facilities.

Solving these problems is difficult. You may find the following ideas helpful.

- Set up a working party of governors to develop a marketing/public relations policy.
- Meet with local heads to discuss and agree on a protocol for dealing with applications from outside reserved areas.
- Make the best of what you have. Have your Prospectus or Information Pack professionally printed.
- Develop a programme of induction evenings and Open Days for prospective parents and friends.
- Make a point of contacting the press each month with "good news". Write the copy yourself and, if possible, enclose black-and-white photographs.
- Try to gain projected numbers from your LEA or Health Authority. This will help you to plan ahead.
- Invite your local playgroup in to enjoy presentations. Extend the invitation to parents for curriculum evenings and social functions with your PTA.

Finally, try to make your school a focus for the community. Evening lettings for yoga, keep fit, brownies and cub scouts will draw people from a wide area. Your displays of children's work and the quality of the environment will influence visitors. They will make judgements about your school and your management of it. Just make sure that the toilets are clean.

OPEN EVENINGS

Good primary practice relies upon sound working relationships between parents and teachers. Many parents give hours of their time to help out in the school day. Others find ways of developing the relationship through Friends' Associations and PTAs. But for most parents, Open Evenings are the most important contact that they have with school.

By law the only requirement for contact between parents and teachers is the notification of the arrangements that are made for them to discuss their child's Annual Report. In practice, of course, all schools want to develop meaningful communication with parents and, more importantly, provide opportunities for parents and teachers to see children's work and discuss their progress whenever necessary.

Most primary schools offer an "open door" policy. Parents know the best times to see their child's teacher or contact the head. We would advise developing a practice which combines the informal with the formal. The school's Information Booklet or Prospectus should give details of when and how to contact class teachers to exchange information, perhaps at the start and end of the day. But there must also be more formal opportunities to discuss children's progress and view the work that the children are doing. In your planning for Open Evenings you will want to consider:

- the best evenings to avoid lettings, popular TV programmes
- a whole-school approach, or year groups on separate evenings
- if children are invited or not
- appointments or "drop-in" arrangements for meetings
- where parents should wait for their appointments
- car parking arrangements
- confidential settings for teachers and parents
- refreshments for parents and teachers
- strategies for awkward customers and those who overstay their time.

The head's role is crucial. You need to be accessible and on the alert to support your staff. NQTs are particularly nervous and need to feel that you can bale them out if they run into difficulty. Some parents will show particular concerns they want to share with you. If you can't solve them within a few minutes, make a further appointment when you have more time and gain the advantage of being able to speak to your classteacher in the meantime.

Finally, do thank the staff for their efforts. Cakes in the staffroom the next morning boost morale as well as low sugar levels from the night before!

OPPRESSION
"Oppressions – racism and sexism – remove us from ourselves. We become a stereotype instead of human beings."
(Ntozake Shange, 1987.)

Oppression can be said to relate to structural differences in the use of power. It is also the experience of being oppressed or oppressing. In your role as head, you would assume that you have a certain amount of power. Your status certainly gives you authority. As such you can challenge oppression exercised through the power of others within your school. You must be aware that the abuse of power can lead to inequality, social injustice, stereotyping and discrimination. It can also result in a reduction in access and life choices. Oppression can only happen if it is supported by oppressive thinking and oppressive behavioural patterns. It can only happen within your school, if you allow it to.

Counter oppression by:
- working to make sure your caring ethos and philosophy are a reality
- ensuring that all your staff value the needs of the individual
- empowering others
- keeping all communication channels active
- developing workable systems to facilitate your awareness of everyday practice throughout the school
- working in partnership with oppressed families
- challenging oppressive practice

- questioning whether or not you oppress
- questioning whether or not you are oppressed.

However exercised and to whatever degree, oppression of any kind, is cruel, brutal and overpowering. Oppression is a misuse of power that disadvantages others. You have a responsibility always to *empower*, never to *oppress*.

OVERHEAD PROJECTOR

Overhead projectors were designed to be operated by people with short bodies, long arms and the ability to read upside-down. The rest of us simply have to learn how to use them. However good your material, poor projector technique can ruin your presentation.

To start with, do you really need to use one? If the answer is yes, then select carefully what you intend to show. Have your slides properly printed and labelled. Place them in plastic wallets in a ring binder to keep them clean and in the right order. Make sure that they are clear and bold. Keep the information on each slide to a minimum.

Next, try out your slides on the projector you will be using. If you are visiting a school or college, check beforehand that the equipment will be set up before you get there. Arrive early to make sure. Check that the machine actually works and that the screen is in the right place. Plug in the projector, find the switch and adjust the focus. Walk to the back of the room and make sure that you can see everything clearly.

If you are a seasoned OHP operator, you'll carry a spare bulb, 5 amp fuse and a duster, just to be on the safe side!

PARENTS

Four Parliamentary Acts are relevant to the increased importance in the role of the parent:

- Education Act 1980
- Education (No 2) Act 1986
- Education Reform Act 1988
- Education Act 1993.

These Acts all seek to promote the importance of parental

influence. A view was generally accepted that schools and teachers had too much autonomy, that the pupils who were produced were not fitted to societal demands, that there was a need to restore social divisions in a homogenous state education system, that schools were not all reaching the required standards of consumerism. These views led to:

PARENTAL INVOLVEMENT – PARENT-POWER

How do you provide what the parents want?
- Consider what you think are their needs.
- Ask them want they want.
- Balance this with your own ideals.
- Have a clear vision.
- Decide what is non-negotiable.
- Decide what is negotiable.
- Respect their rights.
- Communicate.

Believe in your parents.

Parent Power can become Parent-Partnership. It is up to you to promote positive relationships. All will ultimately benefit.

PARENT–TEACHER ASSOCIATION *(See PTA).*

PARTNERSHIP

Partnership is a term used in many aspects of our educational world. It can refer to partnership with:

- the LEA
- the DFEE
- your cluster-group of schools
- other heads
- your parents
- your staff
- Higher Education
- your wider community.

The list is inexhaustible and therefore you need to consider why build partnerships? In any terms, partnership is a contractual relationship between two or more persons. You as head must build supportive relationships with as many bodies and agencies as possible. You cannot work in isolation. If you want a successful school you must relate positively to all parties.

How can you build these partnerships?
- by nurturing a caring ethos and philosophy
- by being welcoming
- by valuing others
- by working positively with all partners
- by empowering others
- by building healthy communication channels
- by being available as appropriate
- by organising and structuring your energies, activities and time.

True partners are equal, different roles notwithstanding. Partnership is about co-operation, collaboration, collectivity and corporation. It is about working together in the best interests of your pupils. Partnership is appreciating the achievements of others: pupils, staff, parents, other schools and colleagues. Partnership is a sharing of ideals, information, tasks and outcomes.

Remember, real partners will also be your allies when you most need them.

PETS

White mice, frogs, guinea pigs, hampsters and stick insects all must have chorused their approval of the 1988 Education Reform Act, which effectively declared an amnesty for all school pets. There is simply no time left for cuddling, stroking and prodding.

Problems tend to land with the head. How are you to avoid the wrath of the caretakers and cleaners who discover stroppy stick insects and frantic frogs making a bid for freedom at the end of the day? Who looks after the rabbit when everyone goes home at the end of the summer term?

Vet all creatures (not literally) who are likely to take up residence in your school. Draw the line at pythons, creatures with large teeth, and goats. Make it clear that all non-human living creatures have to have a patron and mentor – usually the class teacher. Make sure that Health and Safety rules are observed.

Finally, when that particularly difficult governors' meeting has finished at 10.30pm, make a check on one of your furry or scaly friends. You're guaranteed a warm welcome. And you may at last have found someone who will listen to your point of view.

PHILOSOPHY
How well-defined is your philosophy?

Your philosophy is the rationale underpinning your role, and therefore your whole school. It is your educational ideology, your basic beliefs, values and principles. The tenets on which you base your daily being depend on your personal philosophy. Your philosophy foundation was probably formed in college and it has gradually gained structure since. Each educational experience has contributed to your thinking. Every new encounter will help mould your doctrine.

The confidence you transmit to others will be influenced by your "Weltanschauung", your view on the world. All whom you interact with will feel more secure if they can share in your clearly defined school of thought.

How do you develop a sound viewpoint?
- allow yourself time to reflect and think
- observe good practice
- recognise poor practice
- evaluate the distinctions
- research educational theory
- be objective
- discuss and debate
- attend seminars and conferences
- consider the views of others
- be open and flexible
- allow yourself to be challenged.

A secure philosophy will help you survive in headship. You will be able to display equanimity, self-possession, restraint, stoicism and even wisdom, if you are continually clarifying and cultivating your philosophy. While you may hold solid basic beliefs, you and your school will benefit if you are constantly investigating, re-visiting, re-defining and re-building your philosophy.

Your philosophy is your vision: your past, present and future. Your challenge is to make it become a reality for your pupils, staff and you.

PIANOS

Is there a problem with your piano? Does it go out of tune frequently? Does it become a dumping ground for PE shorts, earrings and coffee cups? Is it ruining your hall floor? Make it a feature! Give it a name! The lead singer of the most popular band of the time, or a character in a favourite book or comic is a good idea. Your children will rapidly develop a sense of ownership and care for something which has an identity.

Have it tuned regularly on a contract basis and tell the children when it is happening, so that they can hear the difference. Invest in some large rubber wheels so that it glides smoothly and safely across your shiny hall floor. Ask a parent helper with a penchant for collage or embroidery to make a bright backing cover. Above all, make sure it is played as often as possible. You are bound to have children who would love to play, but don't have an instrument at home. Timetable certain breaktimes when they can come in and play. Ask the children to look after it: give them the polish and the dusters! Your piano will soon become a friend if looked after and cared for.

PLATEAU

Career plateau is all about having reached a level from which you feel that you cannot move or advance. Due to the stage, age or circumstance in which you find yourself, you feel constrained. You might well feel that for some reason or another you have been unable to fully develop your potential. You recognise that you need a new challenge, a change.

More and more heads are experiencing career plateau, because previously available options have diminished due to:
- re-structuring of Local Education Authorities
- reduction in educational expenditure
- changes in teacher training *(See STRESS, MENTORING FURTHER STUDY, THEORISTS.)*

- developments in the inspection of schools
- economic factors
- an increase in fixed-term contracts.

Having negotiated a good salary in your present school, you might not be able to afford to move. Vacant posts are often advertised on low scales with the expectation that the new incumbents themselves will negotiate progressive salary increases. In the current educational climate it you may have to come to terms with the fact that there are fewer career opportunities for heads.

If you are experiencing plateau what can you do about it?
- Come to terms with your situation.
- Be positive.
- Be objective in analysing your perceived needs.
- Try to develop challenge and stimulus in your present post.
- Consider studying Higher Educational courses.
- Set yourself personal aims, objectives and targets.

If you know that you can no longer give of your best, you must seriously consider whether you should stay in post! Having undergone a form of self-analysis, however, you will hopefully feel rejuvenated, and ready and willing to meet the many stimulating challenges awaiting you!

Count your blessings, you may have more than you think!

POLICE

You call them when there are problems. Sometimes they come, sometimes they appear to ignore your requests. Your problem is of gravest concern to you and your school. The police, however, might have more pressing tasks to deal with. By the time they arrive it is often too late. Even so, the presence of a police officer on your site does act as a deterrent factor, in and around the community.

Police officers have various roles to play in relation to your school.

Community police
- are assigned to your school

- visit regularly
- have a quasi-educational responsibility
- should make themselves known to children and staff
- assist in pastoral responsibilities.

In running an effective school you need the support of your local police force. In nurturing well-balanced law-abiding future citizens, you need to establish security and trust between children and all figures of authority.

As in the formation of all relationships there will be times when you:

- are frustrated
- are short of time
- have to intervene
- monitor
- establish a rapport
- clarify your aims.

If you feel that you are building trust, respect and confidence in the police in most of your pupils, then you have succeeded. The life-long benefits to your pupils will be invaluable and are immeasurable.

POLICIES

A policy is a plan of action adopted by you and your staff.

It is:

- an agreed approach
- a course of action
- a guideline
- a procedure
- a programme.

You are required to develop policies to detail various areas of school life. For example:

- curriculum
- assessment
- recording
- reporting
- induction
- staffing
- Pay and Conditions
- Special Needs.

The list is inexhaustible. Basically you need to be able to display that you have analysed and agreed school practice. It is insufficient to verbalise your intentions. Agreed procedures must be recorded. Any theoretical schemes or plans should become common and "real" practice.

Policies will become practice if:

- all staff have been involved in the conception, formulation, development and implementation
- staff feel a sense of ownership
- policies are user-friendly.

Policies will *not* become practice if they are imposed.

Policies *will* become practice if they are agreed.

Policies *will* become practice if someone takes responsibility to ensure that they *do*!

Your policies are testimony to your:
- ethos and philosophy
- curriculum approach
- values
- whole-school development.

Policy-making is your chance to provide an opportunity for your staff to work together. It is an occasion when you can involve them all in decision-making. It can be an advantageous experience for all concerned. One in which you can evaluate your practice and you can proudly commit your shared practice to paper.

POLITICS
If you feel that politics has nothing to do with you, as head, and your school, you could well be deluding yourself. It could be argued that life is a series of political experiences.

The politics of change
Change, or just the possibility of change brings to the fore feelings and emotions that will be otherwise hidden in the day-to-day fabric of the school. Power struggles will emerge in any development or change.

Micro-politics
Micro-politics has been described as "an organisational underworld" (Hoyle 1989). Micro-political issues are those things that many teachers, and heads, would prefer to ignore. (Pretend that they are not there and they will go away!) You as a successful head will be employing micro-political strategies consciously and unconsciously daily. Micro-politics is your

attempt to define your school. It is the power that evolves in your struggle to manage your school effectively.

Macro-politics
Macro-politics are the influences and the power struggles imposed by the State and media in general. You have to respond to and subsequently manage these external controls.

Party politics
Party politics will affect your school in many ways. The Education Acts imposed by the Government of the day will have to be responded to. It is your responsibility to ensure that this happens. Your staff will respond to different directives according to their own political views. The reactions of your parents will also be influenced by their political views. Your own philosophy and ethos will be biased, to a lesser or greater degree, by your personal political beliefs.

How do you manage the politics of your school?
- assertively
- confidently
- by respecting the views of others
- by considering all viewpoints
- by ensuring that your philosophy and ethos is central in all developments and activities.

Whichever way you look at it, the politics of your school are complex. Numerous pressures and forms of power will invade you in your role as head. Your manipulation of conflict and decision-making will impinge on the success of your school.

PONDS
Have you one? A pond of still water artificially created? Whether natural or artificial, if your school has one you need to be aware of:

Potential pond problems
- plastic linings which are susceptible to repeated vandalism
- water encourages uninvited paddlers
- pupil safety
- public safety

- control of pond wildlife and pests
- rapid plant growth
- fertilization of pond-life

If you are considering one, or have a pond already, you need to maximise its potential. In so doing:

- fence, in an attempt to make it safe
- plant shrubs and bushes to provide a screen for privacy and to discourage vandalism.

Consider the implications if pupils are not supervised on pond visits. Ponds are a stimulating and invaluable resource but they are also potential danger zones. You are wise, therefore, if you take all possible safety precautions. Agree a code of conduct with your staff and insist that it is followed at all times.

Ponds are an educational environmental resource that can be used to the advantage of your pupils. Many children never get the opportunity to study and appreciate wildlife first-hand. Whether you have an urban or a country school, you can exploit ponds for positive environmental, scientific and natural educational experiences, addressing both local and global issues. *(See GROUNDS; ENVIRONMENT; FENCES.)*

POST

Letters, circulars and packages are transported and delivered regularly to you. You also dispatch and mail written communications, at times post haste, at others not so promptly! That is the problem: how do you deal with the post you receive and cope with the returns you have to make as a consequence?

One way is to have a clearly defined system:

- Mail is opened and date-stamped by your secretary as the first task of the day.
- Mail is subsequently put on your desk for action.
- Categorise your post.
- Prioritise any action.
- Sort for filing.
- Try to deal with the immediate as soon as possible.
- Be ruthless and "bin" what you can.
- Dictate letters to your secretary.
- Prioritise tasks with your secretary.

- Monitor response times.
- Ensure that both you and your secretary note in diaries, dates of returns etc.
- Plan your time together accordingly.

Time spent in developing a positive relationship with your secretary and clerical staff will reap dividends. A successful team will be one where you will be in tune with each other and your post will be dealt with. Matters will be dealt with systematically and your needs and those of your school will be interpreted as a matter of course. Dealing with the post efficiently and effectively will make for a harmonious and successful school.

POWER
Power can be:

- political
- social
- authoritarian
- privileged
- status
- warranted.

You, as head, exercise power in many areas.

Power is *not* about struggling for control and dominance over others... but *is* created in interaction, with and through others. It is *not* single-minded, one-sided, aggressive, hierarchal, dominating... but participatory, supportive, sharing, built on influencing and networking.

Remember, that those who have power are not necessarily those whom you assume to have it, or those who will use it to the advantage of others.

You may, or may not, be the most powerful being in your school. As head, you have been given authority but power is not a natural pre-requisite of that authority.

You can have:
- authority without power
- power without authority
- both.

A sobering thought for any head... but one that may well encourage you to reflect on the power you wield! Power can be used to the advantage of others in the organisation; or it can be used solely to the advantage of the power-holder. In short, power can be used to the advantage or disadvantage of those within the organisation.

As an inspired head, you will hopefully:
- share power
- experience greater power with others' co-operation.

If you feel you do have power . . . remember: Power shared is power increased.

PRESENTATIONS

As head you will be party to many presentations. You will have to deliver information to colleagues, parental and wider community audiences. You will present yourself in assemblies, curriculum evenings, Inset days, staff meetings, conferences and a variety of other situations.

You will encourage your staff to present their skills in some similar ways.

Your pupils will give presentations of their dramatic and musical skills. Despite the fact that you are likely to have had little or no involvement in its conception, you will feel responsible for the standard of production.

You will feel more confident if you retain a measure of control with pupils and staff. Make sure you:

- view all dramatic productions prior to presentation to wider audiences
- give encouraging but constructive and honest feedback to pupils and staff
- discuss all presentations with the staff involved beforehand
- ensure that you are satisfied with all arrangements, delivery, rendition, performance and subsequent messages.

As head, you are representative of your school and you will be called to account for and judged by everything that happens in it. As such, you will obviously want to feel proud of all connected with it. If you prepare yourself and allow others to do likewise for all presentations, you should be able to feel so.

PROBATIONARY PERIOD

A probationary period is a test period, a trial-time in which you can examine the worth of a new member of staff, a period after which you are not committed to keeping the person in post.

At one time the probationary period for teachers was their initial year of teaching in which there was a commitment to monitor and support the new entrant. During this period the contract could be terminated if the person was deemed to be unsuitable. It also gave probationers the opportunity to exercise their rights in leaving if they felt that either the school or teaching was not for them.

Newly qualified teachers no longer have a probationary year. The ability to make the right appointment in the first place is more crucial now than ever before. No matter how confident you are in your choice, you would be wise to consider the benefits of continuing a support programme.

You do employ many people and it could be to your advantage to employ some on a negotiated initial temporary period.

This is particularly helpful in the case of:
- cleaners
- mid-day meals supervisors
- part-time teachers
- teachers on fixed-term contracts.

Probation can give you the opportunity to examine:
- the contribution of the person selected
- the necessity for such a post
- the needs of the job.

It gives you the chance to respond to changing circumstances. If dissatisfied, either or both parties can take the necessary measures with dignity. You can state your terms for what you expect to happen in a given period.
(See INTERVIEWS, NEWLY QUALIFIED TEACHERS.)

PROSPECTUS

All schools have a Prospectus, although they vary in quality. It is a requirement to produce certain information for prospective parents.

Your Prospectus is:
- anticipatory and hopeful
- a chance to allude to your School Development Plan
- a promise of things to come
- an account
- a landscape for learning
- informative
- visionary.

The statutory requirements of what you have to put in your Prospectus appear to increase annually. Do not let this put you off; your Prospectus is yet another opportunity to share your philosophy with others. For parents, in many cases a browse in, or receipt of, the Prospectus will be the first link with your school. It can initiate interest, hopefully leading to a request for a tour and subsequent pupil registration.

In realizing the importance of your Prospectus, endeavour to keep a balance. Try not to go over the top! Too much information is off-putting and will not be read. Too little is even more frustrating. . . A lavish brochure begs parents to question why you are not spending the money on books, in budget-conscious times!

Your Prospectus:
- should inform
- must attract
- is user-friendly
- is non-jargonistic
- contains simple, concise, clear language
- is interesting.

You do not have to go as far a . . . "a free gift with every copy".

You do however, have to solicit the interest of your prospective parents. . . Your Prospectus is yet another opportunity to . . . SEEK TO WIN.

PROTECTION

As head, you will be concerned to protect all the children in your care. You will be aware that the children may be abused or assaulted. Children can be at risk through external forces or

PROTECTION

even within their own family. You must protect your pupils as much as you can. You must endeavour to prevent abuse, assault or any accidents occurring. It is not easy to do any of these things.

In protecting children you can only do your best in preventing and being alert to signs of possible abuse.

Emotional abuse

You are conscious that a significant number of children are subjected to emotional abuse. Children who are withdrawn, unkempt, irrational or exhibit inappropriate behavioural traits, may be suffering from emotional abuse.

Sexual abuse

Some children are sexually abused by parents, friends or strangers. Pupils who flaunt their bodies, act out sexual behaviour, and use sexual language, may be suffering from sexual abuse.

Physical abuse

Age and size do not act as barriers to those who physically abuse children. Body and facial bruising and burns are all too often signs of such abuse. Pupils who flinch when approached, or those who lack self-esteem, may be suffering from physical abuse.

What can you do?
- Develop links with child support agencies.
- Develop links with the families.
- Always put the needs of the child first.
- Be alert in recognising signs.
- Be aware of your responsibilities.
- Be aware of necessary actions.
- Ensure that all your staff are aware of their responsibilities.
- Have a simple, confidential system of recording any signs of abuse.

Your school may be the only secure and stable component in the life of your pupil at risk. You must, therefore, be very careful to act objectively. If you make an incorrect judgement you may alienate the family and this will have an adverse effect on the child.

Try to help rather than alienate... and acquaint yourself with the Children's and Young Person's Act of 1989.

PTA

Parent Teacher Associations were conceived at a time when there was little opportunity for parents and teachers to meet. Other than entering the school for consultation evenings and concerts, parents rarely went into school. PTAs were formed to give parents and teachers the opportunity to work together in raising funds for their school through social events. They reflected a period in education prior to the Education Reform Act (1988). Teachers, it could be argued, had the time to give and saw this as part of their role. Many parents saw part of their role as a fund-raising one. Post-ERA there seems to be a different climate. With the developing role of the teacher, few have the time or energy to work with the same zeal in PTAs. Most schools have an open-door policy and therefore teachers and parents relate more naturally together. Some PTAs have evolved into pressure groups to argue for better funding.

The ERA also put an onus on schools to relate more to the wider community. This may lead you to question whether or not a Friends' or Community group would better reflect the needs of the school. There are many ways in which to raise money and you need to consider carefully the options best for you. Your responsibilities, as head, have increased manifold and you need to consider what your role will be in any fund-raising group. You represent the school and are therefore accountable for the management of all funds connected to it. This must, therefore, be a consideration. Can you delegate while observing this accountability?

What do you do?
- Consider all the options.
- Agree a constitution for all such groups.
- Make it water-tight regarding roles, responsibilities and management of finances.
- Delegate, cultivate an exofficio role.
- Clarify that involvement is voluntary, not mandatory, for staff.

- Assert the professional role of all teachers.
- Be in control of the type and number of functions held.
- Encourage realism.
- Be in control of what any money is spent on.
- Do not allow funds to be taken off the premises, use the school safe/depository.
- Be a signatory or joint signatory on all cheques.
- Empower, entrust and encourage.

Remember, you can remain in control, no matter how distant your role.

PUBLICITY

To publicise is to gain attention, to advertise or to capture some recognition for your school. In this post-ERA era, publicity for your school may well appeal or even seem essential! It is important to keep your quotient of pupils a healthy one. The only way to do this may be to promote your wares! Remember, however, all publicity is not good publicity! The techniques employed to attract public attention can be successful in drawing attention to your school. Such methods may be unsuccessful in fulfilling your aspirations. In seeking publicity, you naturally wish to promote your school in some way. But never assume this to be a natural outcome!

You must however ALWAYS endeavour for a positive outcome.

In your quest for publicity, always:
- Be guarded in communications with the press, though not so as to make journalists suspicious of you.
- Try not to say anything that can be misconstrued.
- Prepare your own press release if possible.
- Double-check press interpretations of your quotations.
- Know what you actually said.
- Correct press reports as appropriate.
- Be assertive.
- Be in control.

Consider the implications of being in the public eye, whether television, video or newspaper... The power of the media is such that you must be prepared for being misquoted, misrepresented or even exploited!

If you are:
- Do not panic.
- Take it in your stride.

If you take it calmly, then others will do likewise.

Life has a rich pattern that can be woven to your advantage if you remain in control of the thread! Sometimes even unexpected or initially seemingly "bad" publicity can be turned into a blessing if you have the wit to exploit it thus!
(See also MARKETING; MEDIA.)

PUNISHMENT

How often do you feel required to enforce a penalty for a misdemeanour? With what regularity do you have to combat offensive behaviour? Do you ever feel the necessity to treat pupils harshly?

Why do such questions raise alarm bells?

Because as head you desire to cultivate a harmonious school, in which all interact positively together... The reality, however, is a climate where a diverse range of individuals attempt to relate daily together. The result is, often, *dis*harmony!

What sanctions can you enact or enforce? This is your constant challenge, as head and "chief disciplinarian". The answer is: very few! Gone are the days of beatings. Gone are the days when you could rely on the full support of parents and media. In fact, the opposite is probably nearer the truth... Society appears to demand more now of schools than ever before. You have minimal influence over what happens to your pupils out of school hours. External influences are often more powerful than your internal ones.

So what can you do?
- Develop a clear, and considered behavioural policy.
- Involve staff, parents, governors and children in its conception.
- Ensure that everyone receives a copy.
- Ensure that the reward system is clear to all.
- Sanctions for inappropriate behaviour should be known, consistent and fair.
- Discuss behaviour regularly with all staff and children.

- Build a partnership with parents, enlist their support.
- Avoid losing your temper.
- Discourage your staff from shouting.
- Build in systems where children can be removed from potentially "explosive" situations.
- Build in systems where staff can honourably remove themselves to avoid "explosive" situations occurring.
- Encourage staff to take breaks/to unwind.
- Facilitate pupils being given the chance to reflect/to unwind.
- Develop mutual respect and a caring attitude as part of your ethos and philosophy.
- Listen.

Developing in your pupils an understand of what is acceptable and what is unacceptable behaviour is a constant challenge for you as head. Children must accept that there must be penalties for inappropriate behaviour. You must be confident and consistent in your use of sanctions. You must retain the power at all times. Your pupils need to feel secure in your care.

They will if you remain in control.
(See also DISCIPLINE; BULLYING; BEHAVIOUR.)

QUEUES

Queuing is a British characteristic. Queues are symptomatic of war-time and times of shortage or emergency. Your school should not be distinguished by the queues that form within it!

If lines of persons are noticeable around your school:
- Check whether or not they are forming country dance circles.
- Enquire what they are waiting for.
- Queue-jump and send everyone away.

Queues consist of pupils, staff or visitors waiting for something. If they are a regular occurrence in your school, you have a problem. Those in queues are unemployed. Pupils, staff or others are disengaged while waiting to be seen, or waiting to have their needs met in some way. If you notice regular queues of children forming in classrooms, you need to question why this is happening. Queues are a potential breeding ground for disruptive behaviour. Discontent or disruption is not exclusive to children! Queuing adults may well use the time to generate dissatisfaction, anxiety or anger. Children will either "switch off" completely or use the time to create a diversion of some kind!

Consider carefully strategies to alleviate the queuing syndrome:

In the classroom
- Discuss effective teaching and learning strategies with all staff.
- Encourage staff to share individual classroom organisation and management strategies.
- Encourage staff to consider their role as teacher in planning (to consider teacher-intensive tasks/use of time, etc.).
- Encourage planning for extension activities within the curriculum.

At lunchtime
- discuss the effective management of the lunch-break with your midday meals supervisors.

Parents waiting to collect children
- Provide an attractive waiting area with seating.
- Encourage staff to let pupils out of class on time.

Those waiting to see you
- Try to manage your time efficiently and effectively.
- If you are aware of a queue forming, minimise your communications.
- Provide comfortable seating, reading material and the offer of refreshment.
- Endeavour to predict potential queue-formations and in so doing, consider ways of avoiding "bottle-necks".

It is worth remembering:
- Queues are for fairgrounds.
- People queue for buses.
- No one should have to queue for education.

RACISM

Racism is prejudice leading to discrimination by members of one race against another by reason of the difference of race. Though not essential to the definition, it normally involves oppression by members of a dominant racial group of members of a different race based on a false sense of security and confidence in their own racial identity. For obvious historical reasons the commonest form of racism is white over black.

You need to understand the nature of racism in order to address it within your school. Whatever their colour, class or creed, all your pupils are entitled to access a broad, balanced and differentiated curriculum. They must all experience equality of opportunity, as must all your staff and prospective applicants for any vacant posts.

It has often been argued that some white workers use strategies to ignore and deny that racism exists in their workplace. Ask yourself whether or not this is the case in your school?

Your school would benefit if you explored with your staff aspects of:

- denial (racism exists elsewhere)
- colour-blindness (all the same)
- patronage (false acceptance of equality whilst accepting the realities of superiority)
- dumping (placing the responsibility for eliminating racism on black people)
- omission (racism is not important so can be ignored)
- decontextualisation (agreeing that racism operates in general but not in specific daily interactions and routines)
- avoidance (accepting that racism exists but rejecting any responsibility to do anything about it).

You DO have a clear responsibility to do something about it!

Check to ensure that any black pupils or staff are not discriminated against. What choices are given to them? What is their impression of their school experience? Do they display signs of being appreciated and valued? How do you deal with any complaints? Are you confident in redressing unacceptable practice?

Take professional responsibility for any racist incident which takes place in your presence and in so doing challenge in a way you feel appropriate to the situation. It will help if you remember to personalise it to yourself.

You need to put into place policies and procedures and work together as a staff in an anti-discriminatory way. You must, however, come to terms with your own views on racism before confidently encouraging an anti-discriminatory programme. If you really *do* believe that, due to hereditary or other factors, some races are endowed with an intrinsic superiority, *you have a problem . . . and so do your pupils and staff!*

REDUNDANCY

One of the most unpleasant tasks you will have as head is to recognise when staff are supernumerary to requirements. You have a budget to manage and no matter how much you wish to maintain your staffing complement, if you cannot balance the figures, you will have to make cuts. Staffing commands a substantial proportion of the budget and if you cannot make significant reductions elsewhere, you will have to lose staff.

In coming to terms with this fact you will also have to appreciate that there is no easy or pain-free way of dealing with redundancy. In your role as head, unless you can achieve the staff reduction through resignations, staff leaving for other jobs, or selection from volunteers, you will be seen to be responsible for robbing a colleague of their livelihood. You will be involved in the selection process in highlighting who is superfluous.

How do you cope?
- Be flexible enough in your approach to the problem so as to maximise the potential for finding the solution by selection from volunteers.
- Come to terms with the situation.
- Keep at the forefront of your mind that it is a *post* that is redundant and not a *person*.
- Remain objective.
- Follow an agreed code of practice.
- Be prepared for unpleasant atmospheres.
- Fully involve your governors and capitalise on their support.

- Off-load your own feelings to someone you trust and respect.
- Do not take things personally.
- Remain resolute.
- Find a fresh diversion/unwind.
- Be cautious in all communications.

No matter how unpleasant and difficult the task, try not to get personally involved, while at the same time showing the necessary human understanding. When you accepted your post of headteacher, you accepted everything that went with it. This means you took on board the least rewarding aspects of the role as well as most rewarding! Despite the fact that you will be tempted, try not to over-indulge in self-pity. Everyone else will be feeling sorry for themselves and you will be the last person anyone will think of.

No matter how unpleasant, you cannot avoid the inevitable, so get on with it and good luck!

RELATIONSHIPS

All organisations are about people. As head you have to relate to all the different characters who make up your school. You need therefore to develop effective relationships.

Harmonious relationships are vital in making teaching, learning, managing and working together successful.

As head you need to nurture, develop and convey respect.
- You need to let people know that they are valued and that their developing practice is worthwhile.
- Try to make each individual feel important.
- Empathise with your staff, parents and governors.
- Try to understand the point of view of others.
- Be yourself in conveying genuineness.
- Share appropriate feelings sensitively while being conscious of timing.

In building effective relationships you need to be fair, consistent and professional at all times. You will find some individuals easier to relate to than others. It is important, however, that you recognise this in apportioning your interest and time among your staff. Be generous with constructive encouragement to those who do not share your interests and who may even seem to be on a different plane! It could be argued that in order to build cohesive teams of diverse individuals, you need to spend more time with those you do not relate to naturally, than those you feel more comfortable with!

In the formation of effective relationships you will be:
- constantly challenged
- often disappointed and occasionally let down.

Don't let this put you off; the rewards of people working well together are more than worth the effort involved.

RELIGIOUS EDUCATION

Your pupil-intake reflects the ever-changing technological and multi-cultural society in which we live. Your staff will also reflect a diverse range of beings who make up this culture: humanists, Christians, non-believers or followers of other religions or religious sects...And yet, all are required to inculcate a broadly Christian education for pupils while promoting an appreciation of other non-Christian religions and cultures.

How do you meet the requirements while reflecting society?
- Be aware of what is legally required.
- Reflect on the society in which you live and respond.
- Be continuously conscious of the needs of all your pupils.
- Consider the difference between worship and experience.
- Encourage empathy and tolerance.
- Respect the beliefs and non-beliefs of all children and staff.
- Be confident in your philosophy and ethos.
- Always accommodate, tolerate and above all, RESPECT.

REPORTS

You are required to give a written report annually to parents containing certain information about their child's progress. In signing each report, you are endorsing its contents.

In so doing, do you sanction:
- incorrect spellings
- poor grammar
- illegible or untidy handwriting
- subjective comments
- destructive remarks.

Unless you are thorough in checking each report, you could be creating problems for your school. Parents are justified in challenging any of the outlined aspects. Once something is in writing it cannot easily be retracted. A child could be psychologically damaged by an inappropriate use of language.

How do you avoid such problems arising?
- Discuss with staff the importance of report writing.
- Agree appropriate and inappropriate terminology.
- Consider giving each teacher a list of common spelling errors found in previous reports.
- Check every report.
- Insist that mistakes and inappropriate comments are rewritten.

Checking each report is time-consuming but worthwhile. In not allowing poor reports to go out, you are being assertive. You have a responsibility to protect the image of your school and it will become tarnished by mediocre or negative reports. Despite the fact that few, if any, will appreciate it, you are safeguarding staff in stopping them from displaying their inadequacies. You are protecting those who cannot protect themselves: your pupils.

SECRETARIES

The role of Secretary or Bursar has become increasingly high-profile with local management of schools and open enrolment. The job carries more responsibility, the work is harder and demands more time. Although pay has not quite kept up with rocketing status, these jobs attract large numbers of applicants. This probably reflects the high degree of satisfaction that the job brings.

Secretaries need a range of skills: word-processing, reading spread-sheets, managing time and people; as well as a degree of financial acumen. Their exercise can make your secretary appear almost indispensable. Confidentiality and diplomacy are also essential requirements when dealing with politically sensitive issues. But beware the empire-builder. Secretaries acquire a great deal of inside knowledge which gives them a power base. If you're not careful, you may find that your secretary is taking decisions without your knowledge. Or your secretary may be sinking under the pressure, unable to prioritise, making mistakes which you have to correct. Secretaries who can't cope, despite extra help and training, need to go. Your school cannot afford to retain a key worker who is not up to the job, however good they may be with the children.

Avoid these problems by careful recruitment in the first place and then by boundary management. Give your secretary a written job description, specifying in detail the tasks to be done. Answering the phone within four rings and a set patter when receiving guests may seem over the top. But a secretary who allows calls to go unanswered or is rude to visitors is a liability. Make sure that all members of staff, especially your deputy, know what tasks the secretary can, or cannot do.

Have regular meetings, not just to go through the diary, but for you to check that matters are being handled in the way you want. Give your secretary somewhere pleasant to work, with decent furniture, good lighting and ventilation. Arrange regular training. Appraise your secretary at least once every year and consider any advice for improving office routines and systems.

A mutually supportive and respectful relationship between secretary and head is essential for a successful school.

SEXISM

Sexism is the use of sexual stereotyping to treat women and girls differently. It involves the reduction of opportunities which limit the power of females. Sexism is dependent on having power. It is often implicit rather than explicit: the assumption behind the action may not be articulated but the effect on females is the same. Sexual stereotyping has been integrated into organisations in such a way that well-meaning males exercise influence to the disadvantage of females. Men and boys can also experience sexism but the *main* victims tend to be women and girls. It can lead to conformity to gender roles in a way that inhibits the ability, preferences and aspirations of both males and females. This is often done unconsciously!

You must be conscious of sexism within your school and in your dealings with others. *AVOID* subscribing to the premise that you can treat everyone the same! In so doing, you are hiding behind your equal opportunities policy and are indulging in tokenism and paying lip service to the concept of sexism. Equal opportunities is *not* about treating everyone the same. Such a notion could be said to be discriminatory in itself! Your staff, pupils and community members, are individuals in their own right and as such have different needs. It is essential to remember that these needs may well be due to differences in gender, or sexuality.

As head, you have a duty to ensure that the existence of sexism within your school is acknowledged and recognised. In so doing, you may feel afraid of saying or doing the wrong thing. You may well feel de-skilled.

However you can, and must, do something: What?

Address the issues:
- Involve all your staff.
- Back policy statements with action plans.
- Review regularly to make theory practice.
- Monitor.

Act:
- Challenge your own prejudices.
- Allow others the opportunity to do likewise.
- Ensure that all staff are aware that sexist language and behaviour will not be tolerated, and why.
- Build in structures to review practice regularly

Explore and challenge:
- preconceptions, assumptions, and judgements
- sexual stereotyping.
- reactions.

Sexism must be addressed at all levels of school life. This means within the *classroom* as well as within the *staff-room*.

SEXUAL HARASSMENT

Anything a person finds upsetting, offensive or embarrassing sexually can be defined as sexual harassment. Harassers are often unaware of their behaviour as being offensive. In some cases, however, it is deliberate. In others, it is acquired behavioural patterning generally accepted in society.

No one should experience sexual harassment of any kind. You have a duty to ensure that it does not take place in your school. If it does then you must do something about it.

What is sexual harassment?

Sexual harassment can range from sexist "jokes" to sexual assault. It is repeated offensive behaviour. It will include: unwanted non-verbal advances, sexually discriminatory remarks and sexually explicit derogatory statements.

Sexual harassment will cause people to feel:
- humiliated
- threatened
- bothered
- patronised.

Sexual harassment will ultimately interfere with the performance of the person being harassed. They will feel that their job security has been undermined. An intimidating and threatening environment will be created within your school. You cannot allow sexual harassment of any kind to take place, develop or flourish within your organisation. Sexual harassment impinges on the rights of the individual. Never undervalue the feelings of others; if someone is offended by sexual innuendo, they have a right to feel thus.

In examining this issue, question whether or not you could be accused of sexual harassment? If you suspect that you could, then do something about it! Seriously consider the messages you transmit in your verbal and non-verbal behaviour.

SPORTS DAYS

Ever since the "back to basics" campaign, designed by politicians to put the "great" back into Britain, school sport has been under the microscope. Blame for our poor performances at national and international levels, in everything from athletics to cricket, has been laid at the door of the education system. And primary schools are most to blame because of their woolly thinking about equality, and anti-sexist games and development of skills, as opposed to competitiveness. Traditionalists will bluster about girls being allowed to play football and competition being a dirty word. What happened to weekly soccer matches after school? Mr Bloggs would pile the whole team into his Morris Minor and off they'd go!

But the world has changed for teachers: accountability, the demands of the National Curriculum, our relationships with parents and children. And sport has changed too. Television and sponsorship on a huge scale has turned Roy of the Rovers into an icon. Win At All Costs is the name of the game.

Sports Days in primary schools should be about keeping as many children challenged and active as possible. Gone are the days of heats and finals, where a few children have the chance to run and the winners are almost always known in advance. Gone are the days when children sat on damp grass, waiting to be tied at the ankle to each other, placed in a sacks, or given an egg and spoon to play with for 100 yards.

Many schools now favour continuous carousel-type activities. Children are placed in mixed-age teams and spend five or ten minutes gaining team points on a whole range of activities. Teachers and parents jot the points down on score-cards. The children help each other and everyone is busy all the time, working at their own level. There's plenty to watch and no time for children to become bored. It satisfies the team sport and competition fanatics. Oh . . . and the children enjoy it too!

STAMINA

Problems with stamina result from not being fit for the job. The primary head needs to be physically and mentally fit. Be selfish for once. Carve out some time every week for regular physical exercise. Make it an essential part of your work and never be tempted to arrange an open evening or governors meeting in place of squash night or aerobics.

Read some fiction every week. Visit art galleries. Do something for yourself which will feed the soul. *(See DIET; CHARISMA; MANAGEMENT.)*

STRESS

You will experience stress at some time. In meeting the demands of your everyday existence you are likely to experience a level of stress. Stress can be a pro-active force, be acceptable and even enjoyable. Too often, however, it is an unwelcome, uncomfortable and unpleasant experience.

This happens when there is an imbalance between your demands and your capability to respond. It is therefore essential to prevent this from occurring. If it does, then you need to have ways of dealing with your stress.

So how can we do this?

- Have a vision.
- Be confident of your values.
- Cultivate and nurture an ethos.
- Practice assertiveness.
- Develop your interpersonal skills.
- Delegate.
- Manage your time effectively.
- Be aware of your diet.
- Keep fit.
- Believe in yourself.
- Have a support system.

How can you avoid or manage stress?

By remaining objective and standing back from the problem. No matter how worried you are, try to laugh it off with a joke. Shrug it off: "Oh, well. . ." Look for positives.

Focus on something else. . . DEFER, DISPLACE, DELEGATE, DELAY.

Ask yourself, "How important is this in the scheme of things?"

Be nice to yourself. Treat yourself. Escape for a while. Reflect and relax. Prioritise.

Remember, if you want to be an effective head, you need to be happy and calm. So learn to unwind and leave your problems behind. Who knows, they may not be there in the morning. And if they are, well address them then!

STUDENTS

The onus on schools to play an increasing role in the training of teachers can place heavy demands upon mentors and class teachers. Even with able and hard-working students, schools have to put in time and effort in support. Most colleges and universities pay schools for placements: but the income rarely matches the costs. Teachers take on students as part of their commitment to the profession. They use the opportunity to pass on some of the skills of the craft of teaching. They may also pick up something new in the process. But having a student for a six-week block is hard work. Assessment, routines and behaviour can all suffer – and the class teacher then has to work very hard to bring everything up to scratch.

Problems with students on teaching experience can cause havoc. The following points should help:

- Look carefully at the contract that you have with the university. Make sure you agree and that the staff as a whole understand what the school's commitment is.

- Before the practice starts, spell out your expectations to the student: time-keeping, dress, planning and preparation, confidentiality, attendance at staff meetings – all need to be covered. Do you have a staff handbook?

- Choose wisely where you will place the student. Placing a student with a poor teacher, in the hope that something may rub off, is disastrous for everyone.

- Make sure that you actually tell your teacher!

- Don't allow things to ride. Tackle problems head-on, when they occur.

- Agree the dates of visits with the university tutor, well in advance.

- Either you, or a senior member of staff, should meet weekly with the student, to look at written plans and records.

- If things go drastically wrong – pull out! Students who are failing, despite support, either need another placement or another career. Your children and staff shouldn't have to suffer. As a primary head, your key task is about the teaching of children, not teacher training.

(See INITIAL TEACHER TRAINING, MENTORING.)

SURVIVAL

The essential change in the role of the primary head since the Education Reform Act has been the shift away from the role of the "leading professional" to that of "business manager". The management of time, people and money are at the heart of the job. But many problems faced by heads will stem, not from having to cope with the new role, but from *not* having the training to do so.

"Headteacher Stress, Coping and Health" (Ostell and Oakland, 1992), studied a sample of primary heads in Bradford. The focus was the amount of stress revealed in 80 heads in first and middle schools. One of the key findings was that heads felt they never, or only rarely, received training in the skills needed for their new role. Three specific areas of training need were identified:

- Technical skills, including budget planning and general financial management.

- Interpersonal skills, including the development and management of teachers and other staff.

- Skills of stress and conflict management.

Management of a school demands that you use many skills. If you have not had training, make sure that you invest in some. Being given responsibility and opportunity as a deputy is not enough. The role of the head is a more isolated one, where personal responsibility has to be felt before it is learned.

To overcome the isolation, make sure that you can network with other heads. Arrange time out to share problems and solutions. Set up a group with others whom you trust. Give it a name if you feel guilty about being out of school over a lunchtime. Not only will your health be safeguarded but you also stand to be a more competent and effective headteacher. You will survive . . .

TEACHERS

Teachers are your most important resource. The fundamental role of a teacher is to help others learn. Children's futures, lives, liberty and happiness are in the hands of your teachers. You cannot over-estimate how much is at stake. You, as head, are also a teacher. You are also responsible to all.

A teacher's role is a demanding one. It is, therefore, essential that you make the best appointment when a vacancy occurs. Under your inspired leadership your teachers will make your school what it is. It is up to you to manage your teachers with dedication, competence and success. While being a realist, you also need to come to terms with the fact that the essence of your school, the philosophy and ethos, will be generated from you as head. Your teachers can only be as good as you allow them to be. You will cultivate the sense of challenge, standards, opportunity and satisfaction in the achievement they experience.

So how do you get the best out of your teachers?
- Create a vision.
- Nurture a team-spirit.
- Generate a sense of ownership.
- Have regular planned and structured staff meetings.
- Involve, empower and encourage.
- Ensure comfortable, secure and safe working conditions.
- Develop the potential of each individual.
- Compliment and congratulate.
- Be honest.
- Nurture a climate of honesty and value.
- Be constructive.
- Set realistic but high standards for yourself and others.
- Reward.
- Encourage a sense of humour.
- Be alert to feelings.
- Celebrate all achievement.

Above all, you need to be sensitive and understanding and nurture a sense of enjoyment in teachers and children.

THEORISTS

Headship can be a lonely experience. Your responsibilities are ever-increasing. You are totally accountable for every action in your school.

If you need to speculate, formulate, hypothesize, project and propound, if you need to assume, presume and surmise, to whom do you refer when you need guidance? To *an educational theorist*. No matter how gifted, very few heads can do very many things unaided. In order to survive, you must *continue* to:

- question
- research
- examine
- analyse
- evaluate.

In order for theory to become practice, you need to make the above REALITY.

You may be inspired by the challenges of P.F. Drucker, the insights of Christian Schiller, the vision of Michael J. Fullan.

Other theorists may well inspire you, as much as, or more than these three. But, whoever you refer to, do continue to research, question, analyse, reflect and THINK. *(See Bibliography and Further Reading.)*

TIME MANAGEMENT

You are more than aware of what you should do, but it is easier said than done. You are, however, responsible for your use of time and everyone will benefit if you use it effectively. If you feel that you are not an efficient time-user, try to evaluate when, how and why you do not use time to advantage.

Do you?
- set priorities
- have targets and goals
- make decisions
- respond pro-actively
- gossip
- say too much
- say too little
- over-commit yourself
- delegate

- have confidence in others
- organise
- keep your diary up to date
- keep your secretary informed
- say NO!

Be honest in your answers. Try not to be too hard on yourself, however much you feel you do *not* achieve. Focus on what you *do* achieve and then decide to go for *more*. Set yourself realistic goals. Take time to think about your performance objectively. Decide what you feel to be effectual practice and then consider whether or not you are a productive person. Your staff and your school will benefit if you are effective. You will benefit if you learn to manage yourself, as well as others! Very few people, if any, really feel that they use time well. You can only do your best, which is what you would expect of your pupils and staff. So start now.

Manage your time; do not let time manage you...

TOILETS

Toilets may not seem very important in the educational scheme of things. If you reflect, however, they are very significant to the daily smooth-running of your school. All children and staff deserve a clean, secure, comfortable and hygienic environment. Decent toilets are central to this.

Children are often reluctant to use school toilets for a variety of reasons. They may be dirty, smelly, have no locks or be short of toilet-paper. As private places, they may well be places where other children can intimidate or threaten.

Staff toilets are often used by hirers and are therefore susceptible to mistreatment or over-use. All staff are entitled to hygienic lavatory conditions. Unsavoury or broken toilets can adversely affect a busy teacher's attitude to work. When you are in a hurry, lack of toilet-paper could just be the last straw!

So what can you do?
- Check all toilets regularly.
- Be clear in your expectations of your caretaker and cleaners.
- Instill respect in children and staff.

- Ensure that plumbing jobs are done as soon as possible.
- Make your toilets attractive places to be in.

By the way, the toilet might be your only refuge as head. The one place you can be alone.

TOURS

Open enrolment has given the tour of the school an increased significance.

Parents will exercise their right of choice in visiting several schools and will not automatically send their child to the school in their reserved area. They will look for the one that meets their requirements. They will select the one that seems to fulfil their aspirations for their child.

Your role as head is an increasingly demanding one. You might feel that tours of your school can be delegated and your time used more fruitfully. This may well be the case. Many parents will visit several schools and the time spent in giving tours will be unproductive. Your school will not always be chosen. You have used valuable time to no obvious advantage and your desk is still groaning under the weight of waiting paperwork. Despite this, consider very carefully before you take the decision to delegate this task.

You will lose:
- the opportunity to share your ethos and philosophy
- the chance to share your educational values
- time to discuss your aspirations for the children and staff in your care
- an opportunity to see everyday practice in your school
- the opportunity to expect your staff to treat tours as important
- the expectation for staff to deliver quality education at all times
- a chance for children to welcome visitors whilst feeling secure
- a special time for children and staff to share their achievements
- a growing pride in your school exhibited by everyone in it.

Remember, every interaction makes an impression. Every successful tour provides a pupil for your school. Pupils bring revenue and make your school a viable concern. Without pupils you would not have a school and you could not continue as a head. Ask yourself, just how important is your next tour?

TRAINING

For many years, teachers were educated, but currently they are trained. This naturally has implications for you, as head, as you will have to undertake a measure of involvement in this training. You will have to ensure that students are coached, disciplined, guided, instructed and schooled in the craft of teaching! You may well be a training establishment for other students in Child Care training and as such you will have to acknowledge your responsibility in accepting apprentices and any would-be scholars.

Any form of training implies tutelage, which in itself suggests a partnership, with each partner undertaking a commitment to the development of the learning experience. In so doing, you need to be fully aware of what is expected of you and your school in order to meet the objectives of the training course. You also need to ensure that your staff do not take on more than they can cope with. Finally, before you agree to host student placements, seriously consider the effect on pupils. Their interests must be your primary concern and if you are confident that they will ultimately benefit, then go ahead.

In order to avoid potential complications, consider:
- agreeing with your staff what is expected of students
- agreeing with staff what is expected of them, as would-be trainers
- being fully aware of shared responsibilities between college and school
- ensuring that students understand the agreed expectations
- checking that all participants are clear about their role and its relation to your school and the particular training programme.

Whether you believe students should be trained or educated, once you are satisfied with the arrangements, go ahead and welcome your trainee. To be involved in the training of any students can be an honourable and uplifting experience for all parties concerned. *(See MENTORING; STUDENTS; INITIAL TEACHER TRAINING.)*

TRESPASSERS

Trespassers are intruders who invade the privacy of your school in some way. In consequence, the security of your pupils, staff and the safety of your site and building is encroached. Whichever way you look at it, trespassers are unwelcome visitors. Somehow or another, you have to stop any transgressors!

How do you do this?
- Enclose your site with adequate fencing.
- Plant prickly shrubs around the perimeter.
- Install security lighting if funds allow.
- Train your caretaker to be vigilant in checking the building at regular intervals.
- Encourage a type of neighbourhood-watch system with your school's immediate neighbours.
- Keep all un-staffed doors closed during the school day.
- Ensure that all visitors sign in and wear a visitor's badge.
- Do not allow any persons to approach children or staff on the playground or within the school, without having gone through an agreed administrative procedure.
- Apprehend if appropriate.
- Inform your local police immediately of any trespassing.

Your children and staff have a right to feel happy and secure when at school. If there is any infringement of this secure environment, you must take assertive action to ensure that it stops. Trespass is not a criminal offence in itself but damage to property and forced entry are criminal acts. Although you may wish to prosecute, the police are obliged to take into account the age and previous history of the offender. In many cases the police will caution, but you have a right to expect criminal proceedings to be taken against repeat offenders.

TRUANCY

Schools have always had truants: pupils who go absent without leave.

However, you are now more accountable for your truants, like everything else. You have to record and publish all unauthorised absences. No matter how you do this, figures in this category do not reflect well on your school. For whatever reason, you are not succeeding. You need to consider why Jamie or Annabelle do not attend regularly. Does it reflect on your staff, your pupils or you? Be objective and honest in your answers.

What can you do about it?
- Evaluate the curriculum offered: is it stimulating and challenging?
- Consider pupil:work "match".
- Examine the atmosphere in relevant classes/the whole school.
- Research whether intimidation is taking place.
- Dig deep into all aspects of a child's school life.
- Make contact with the home.
- Try to build trust with parents/guardians.
- Involve external agencies as appropriate.

Having made an honest assessment of the situation, endeavour to do something about it. Be realistic, however, in what you can achieve. First and foremost must come the needs of the truanting child. Be welcoming and openly supportive of your pupil, who needs your help. Truants are insecure and somehow you have got to offer a form of security. You must build a sense of trust. Try to be understanding. Empathise. Involve your staff, get their support. If a teacher is adding to the problem, do something about it. The child must always come first! Liaise with the support agencies and parents; work in partnership to solve the problem.

You can only do your best. If you have honestly done that, do not see it as failure if you do not succeed. You cannot win them all. *(See also ABSENCES.)*

TRUST

Have you confidence in, and can you rely on others? Have they got faith in you?

Trust is about:
- duty
- obligation
- placing one's confidence in another
- integrity
- guardianship
- dependability
- honour.

If trust can be placed in you, you will be rewarded by being able to consign your trust in others. This will be your reward. As head, however, you must be careful not to be gullible. You must be wary and careful in whom you place your trust.

There are varying degrees of trust and you need to be aware of this. If as a staff you *are* a team, you should be able to take everyone at face-value. You should be able to have faith in their commitment to the ethos, philosophy and values of your school. You should be able to rely on them all to be responsible and caring. You should be able to delegate in sharing responsibility for the development of the school.

You would hope to be able to trust your governors. You need to be able to presume a degree of governor-trusteeship. You need to be able to rely on their confidence and confidentiality.

But you cannot expect to:
- bare your soul
- be naive
- be unguarded, or unsuspecting.

You must be level-headed at all times. Never expect too much of others! You cannot expect others to take over the burden of headship for you. *You* must always remain in control. Be wary in whom you trust! Trust has a fine balance. But to overburden others with areas that should be in your control will destabilise them. You will lose their faith.

To whom do you talk ?
You will find that you *can* confide in someone with whom you feel empathy and have a rapport. Seriously consider whether or not to confide in your partner. To do so may well be your salvation. On the other hand, it could mean that you lose your sanctuary. Your life at home could become affected by school matters, to the detriment of family-life.

If your confidant is someone other than your partner, you can unburden yourself before going home; forget your problems while at home unwind with your family

UNDER-ACHIEVERS
You have a duty, as head, to develop the potential of all pupils and staff within your care. In so doing, you will become aware of the differing abilities, aptitude and achievement of all with whom you relate.

If you suspect, or indeed know, that pupils or staff are under-achieving, you need to consider carefully what you are going to do about it.

Pupil under-achievement can be due to:
- a lack of differentiation within the curriculum
- poor self-esteem
- unhappiness
- lack of stimulation and challenge
- curriculum mis-match
- innate inability
- other reasons.

A clearly defined assessment procedure is essential in the identification of needs. Agreed trialling of pupils' work also enables you to set standards for pupils of the same and differing abilities. If in your planning process you encourage teachers to clearly define their learning objectives and also to state a measure for each task, it will be easier to evaluate pupil achievement.

It is important to evaluate the level of achievement of all children. It can be easy to become satisfied with the able and more-able pupils' output. All children should be stimulated and challenged by the curriculum you offer them in your school.

Under your inspired leadership and school management, all children and staff can reach their true potential. In most cases, you have the power to assist them to achieve this aim.

VANDALISM

Vandals: can you recognise them? Are they ex-pupils? What are you going to do about them?

Schools are targets for vandals and you are expected to do something. You may well have a caretaker, one to whom you give very clear instructions. But what do you do if your caretaker feels threatened or intimidated by interlopers or external pressure and hides in the stockroom, insisting that the mobile phone does not work. . .

How do you take control?
- Call the police.
- Mean business.
- Encourage a neighbourhood watch and enlist the help of pupils, parents and your wider community within, and out of, school hours.
- Encourage your caretaker to act assertively in responding appropriately.
- Install security measures if appropriate.
- Use "anti-vandal" paint on all perimeter walls and fences.
- Plant "unfriendly" spiky bushes around your site perimeter.
- Be assertive but fair in dealing with all vandals, known or unknown to you.

Nurture a trust in the hirers of your building, instilling a sense of ownership and responsibility in others as well as yourself. You need to be constantly alert but considered in your reactions, avoiding judgements. Try to remain calm and assertive in all situations. Question why there is vandalism. Whatever the answer, protect your children and staff by always being one step ahead of your vandals. Do not let them challenge *you*. . . You challenge *them*.

VALUE-ADDED

What advantage or benefit can you give each one of your pupils? How do you measure any merit? Historically, value-added is associated with profit and cost. It is arguable that this cannot be measured in schools. Whether or not this is true, schools are increasingly required to give value and to prove their worth.

Measure what your pupils bring to school.

Despite the fact that it is time-consuming, it is essential to undertake a form of base-line assessment. All subsequent assessments can then be measured against this starting-point. Visual, auditory, motor, language, numeracy and social skills need to be analysed and assessed. The resulting information will shape your individual programme for each pupil. This defines the basis to which you ADD!

How do you do this?
- Record and report pupil progress in *all* areas.
- Set high, achievable and realistic standards.
- Publicly celebrate your achievements.
- Manage your budget to advantage.
- Formally measure progress – SATS/reading tests, etc.
- Develop your pupils' potential – aesthetically, academically, physically, morally and spiritually.
- Be accountable.
- Determine to increase the self-esteem of staff and pupils.
- Nurture above-average practice.

Be confident in promoting your ideals, while manipulating societal demands to the advantage of your pupils.

VIDEOS

It could be said that video-tapes have revolutionised the use of television in recent years. Media studies can be exploited successfully to enhance the educational and leisure experiences of your pupils in school.

You can minimise or even avoid problem areas if the necessary precautions are kept. Video is an invaluable medium and as such its exposure will stimulate your pupils. As in the use of all resources, you need to agree an approach with your staff, in considering the use of all video equipment.

Initiate a system to:
- approve all video-tapes before screening
- ensure that video and television are not being used at the expense of direct experience
- consider participatory tapes if appropriate
- retain control of any filming by spending time discussing content beforehand
- weigh up carefully the pros and cons of potential disruption to the school day
- always put the needs of your pupils first
- insist on viewing any film before it is shown to the public
- consider your objectives in sanctioning any film-making.

Video will enrich the educational experience of your pupils. A creative approach in video film-making could just be an inspired marketing technique for promoting your school. Think about it.

VISITORS

You are subject to many persons who make visits (with or without a card). Visitors, in preferred terms, are guests or invited callers. In real terms, they are people who just "turn-up"/call on the off-chance/inflict their company upon you. However they make their entry into your school, you would be wise to consider an approach to your visitors. Whether invited, or uninvited, all visitors will make a judgement on your school and you want that to be as favourable as possible! You would do well to have a contingency plan for the visitors who just turn up; the ones you cannot deal with because of other commitments.

What provisions do you make?
- discuss with staff an agreed approach to visitors
- develop a corporate responsibility for the school
- be realistic
- develop a basic everyday level of good practice in teaching, cleaning and in interpersonal skills in *all* staff.

If all staff appreciate the value of developing good practice at all times, a good impression will be made. If staff and children become used to welcoming visitors, they will be constantly enhancing their interpersonal skills. The educational experiences of the children will continue, as visitors share in the daily life of your school. The needs of your pupils should always come first and therefore no visits should be disruptive to them.

Consider the importance of your various visitors.

Do you have a different approach to the visit by your local Member of Parliament from that by a prospective parent? Who is the most important to the continuing success of your school? If you practice equal opportunities, you will treat all visitors the same. In so doing, you will treat all visitors *well!* Visitors give you a superb opportunity to share your good practice. Regular visitors give your staff and children the chance to be appreciated by others. If you are relaxed and confident in showing visitors around, then staff and children will be too. You will all enjoy welcoming others!

What do you do if things do not go smoothly?

There will be days when the unexpected happens! If it does, then remain calm and, as always, put the children first! Visitors are usually very impressed to witness difficult situations being dealt with. Be yourself, keep a sense of perspective and a sense of humour!

And remember:

Your school should be a secure environment at all times. Have you a Visitors' book? Do you request all "guests" to wear badges? Think about the consequences if you do not.

VOLUNTEERS

During the course of the school year, you are likely to have a significant number of volunteers, a variety of persons who offer their services to your school. In theory such proposals may seem very attractive; in practice this is not always the case. In accepting offers of help, as a representative of your school, you too are putting yourself at the disposal of another! Volunteers will always have a reason, a need or a hidden agenda in putting themselves forward. The basis for volunteering could be wholly genuine, but in accepting offers of help, you are, to a degree, taking on the responsibility for another person. You may feel indebted in some way.

In deploying volunteers consider:
- how you will use them
- do you need them?
- who will supervise/monitor them?
- how will they relate to the children in your care?
- insurance
- break-time arrangements
- relationships
- boundary management
- long/medium and short term planning
- police clearance (if applicable).

The welfare and security of your pupils must be your first priority, as must be the smooth running of your school. As head, however, you do have a responsibility to the wider community and you can nurture successful partnerships by involving others in the daily life of your school. Voluntary help can be a mutually beneficial experience if you have a planned approach to their contribution. A clearly defined code of practice will benefit all contributors.

VOUCHERS

Most primary heads agree with the principle of nursery education. However, recent proposals to introduce a voucher system will have significant implications for all primary schools with nursery classes. The provision of a high-quality entitlement against a background of market forces will provide major challenges for primary headteachers and their governing bodies.

Proposals:
- a national system of nursery vouchers to be introduced from April 1997.
- phase 1 for "volunteers" will be from April 1996.
- a voucher will be issued on application to parents of a child in the term following the child's fourth birthday.
- the indicative value of these vouchers will be £1,100 per annum, per child.

Implications:
- impact on budgets
- identification of eligible children – pupil-count
- role of your Governing Body
- potential inequality of access if your school is already full
- accommodation issues
- involvement of the private and voluntary sectors
- effect on your future roll
- staffing
- administration.

Whether you view this initiative favourably or unfavourably, you need to:
- retain your vision and commitment
- recognise any constraints
- be pragmatic
- cultivate a positive but realistic approach.

VOYEUR

Most schools unfortunately have one, at some time or another:. a man or woman who derives pleasure, or even sexual gratification, from the observation of others.

You as head, need to combat such undesirable traits. Consider the effect upon children, staff (and you) if someone:

- regularly watches your pupils at work or play
- comments on their activities
- takes photographs
- complains about the school's use of break-times
- is often visible.

What do you do?
- consider the needs of your pupils
- evaluate the security of your whole school
- consider the needs of your staff.

You must act in a measured way in order to combat such repulsive behaviour. Children and staff need to be secure in school at all times. No matter how brief, unsolicited observation threatens. Regular voyeurism of any kind is intimidatory and must therefore be challenged!

Voyeurs have all sorts of reasons for watching children. They may not all be of a sinister origin. Voyeurs can be lonely men or women who simply derive some form of pleasure from watching children at play. This can be acceptable as long as it does not become regular or prolonged. You cannot afford to take chances. If someone is seen watching children for a significant length of time, you need to take some form of action. You might well decide to calmly challenge the observer yourself. On the other hand, a phone-call to the local police may be your choice. If you deliberately make yourself visible at lunchtimes or after school, you can act as a deterrent; as can the police.

Disenchanted parents may adopt the role of "voyeur" for varying reasons. They might not want particular children playing with their own child. They might not like children picnicking on the school field in the summer-time. They might want to gather evidence of in the form of photographs of disputable school practice. Whatever their justification, this type of behaviour is menacing for children and staff. No matter how complex the problem you must deal with it. Voyeurism of any kind can have alarming consequences. So never ignore, always act.

BE ASSERTIVE . . . PROTECT . . . WIN.

WITCHES

Beware of witch-hunts! Be careful not to blame any organisational failure on any marginal or weaker persons within your school even if they *are* trouble makers. In so doing, you may be avoiding taking responsibility for making unpopular decisions and for unaccomplished goals. But ultimate responsibility for the development of the school and the behaviour of those within it is yours alone. If change is taking place, you must be the agent. Make sure you don't find yourself in a position where you blame others for unwelcome or unplanned change.

How to avoid the need for scapegoats?
- Share your goals with all staff
- Encourage those who support your ideals
- Confront inappropriate behaviour

- Challenge dissent
- Keep a sense of perspective
- Remain objective
- Expect gossip and rumour and keep communication channels open to counter it.

Modern witches are no longer burnt at the stake. However, if scapegoating occurs, consider to what extent it needs to be dealt with, if at all.

XMAS

Short for Christmas, the festive season, when Christians celebrate the birth of Jesus. Xmas has also evolved into a secular celebration when greetings and gifts are exchanged. However you view it, it is a very special time in schools. Do you welcome Xmas, or dread it? It depends whether or not you remain in control.

A coping strategy for Xmas with your pupils:
- Agree with your staff your school approach to Xmas.
- Agree a date to initiate preparations.
- Agree a balance of secular and religious content.
- Consider the display and its post-Xmas adaptation.

In meeting the needs of all your pupils, be aware of non-Christian or other groups in your planning. It will be to your advantage to discuss any proposed festivities with their parents. If approached in a certain way, the offspring of such groups might well be able to make a positive contribution to the main part of the curriculum. At the same time you can agree with parents any activities that are inappropriate and they can then make the necessary arrangements.

A coping strategy for Xmas with your staff:
- Wait for staff to propose any in-house gatherings.
- Consider the nature of any suggestions.
- Take part, if you can, on *your* terms.
- Be fair and equitable.
- Seriously consider the wisdom of gift-giving. (Are you head, or Lord/Lady of the Manor?)

Xmas is celebrated annually. You need to question why so many

dread this nationally-esteemed festive season. If you wish to avoid heaving a sigh of relief when it is all over:
- Keep things in perspective.
- Ensure a balance.
- Consider the importance of curriculum continuity.

Above all, Xmas should be FUN. It can be if, as always, you remain in control. Enjoy it with your children, staff and parents. "Joyeux Noel"!

YOUNGSTERS

Girls . . . boys . . . young hopefuls. The future generations of our society.

You are responsible for the youngsters in your school. It could be said that you have their future in your hands. Most new entrants, whether in reception or transition, do have hope. It is in everyone's interest if they retain that hope.

How do you capitalise on this?
- Nurture a positive and caring ethos and philosophy.
- Develop a challenging and stimulating curriculum.
- Be consistent in any system of sanctions and rewards.
- Be clear in your realistic but high expectations.
- Build a partnership with parents and guardians.
- Endeavour to agree on common aims.
- Initiate healthy relationships between youngsters and staff.
- Initiate healthy relationships with the wider community.

Be consistent in dealing with your youngsters. Any sanctions for inappropriate behaviour should be fair. All youngsters should be given the opportunity to redeem themselves. Treat each day as a new one; one where renegades can start afresh. Reward, applaud and encourage whenever you can. Encourage all your staff to do likewise. Value your young hopefuls. . . You have their future in your hands today. They are your future tomorrow.

ZEAL

How often are you filled with, or inspired by, intense enthusiasm? How fervent are you in the achievement of the aims of your school? How well do you manage zealousness in others? Do you capitalise on the inspiration of your staff and parents? Or do you ever allow enthusiasm to become fanaticism? Do you allow yourself to be dominated by ardent causes? Do you jump on bandwagons? Are you prey to the zealot? To immoderate or extreme pressure? Can you recognise extremism?

Seriously consider how you manage a diverse range of individuals.

You can only do this if you:
- are secure in your own philosophy and beliefs
- listen, and consider the views of others
- analyse
- evaluate.

In your role as head, you are responsible for an organisation. The organisation is your school and as such there will be many contributors to this institution. Somehow you must contrive to handle all participants successfully. You must wield the power invested in you and exercise control in the best interests of your pupils. As an administrator, leader and manager, you need to bring out the best in children, staff, parents and the wider community.

You have a responsibility to protect your charges from any extremism. In so doing, your skill is to make all feel valued to a lesser or greater degree. Extremist views or behaviour might well be modified if you ensure that viewpoints have at least been considered rationally and objectively. You may even possess the ability to influence to your way of thinking (which must always be in the interests of your pupils).

Zeal, zealousness and zealots can be dangerous. Fanaticism of any kind is worrying. Be careful, however, not to over-react. You will not, if you remain objective, rational *and* always put the interests of your pupils first.

ZONES
Two very different kinds of zones pose challenges to the primary head. The first concerns the heating in your building;

and the second, the quality of teaching that goes on within it. Both are important . . . but unrelated.

Heating your building in the winter is a costly business. If you have evening lettings, you will only need to heat parts of it. If you are in a local management scheme, where the LEA is responsible for the boiler plant, insist that zone valves are fitted to achieve energy efficiency. This means that when your school is used for Step Aerobics on a Wednesday evening, only your hall needs to be heated. Everyone will be so hot and exhausted that they won't notice that the entrance hall and the toilets are freezing cold.

The "Zone of Proximal Development" belongs to Leonid Vygotsky. Jerome Bruner re-defined it as the "Zone of Potential Development". Both Vygotsky and Bruner describe the intervention of the teacher at critical stages in the child's learning to achieve greater understanding. They describe the concept of "scaffolding" – a building of skills and concepts by the teacher – which enables the child to make an independent leap in understanding.

Both zones are important. But saving money on the first will never match the value you add in the second.

ZOOS

Once upon a time a zoo visit constituted the annual school excursion. A joyous trip to the place where live animals are kept, exhibited to the public, studied and bred.

After the 1988 Education Reform Act, any visit to the zoo will be part of the studied theme or received curriculum. For whatever reason your children do venture forth, you will be wise to remember the following:

- 'The Lion and Albert'
- rules about touching animals
- rules about feeding animals
- inclement weather contingencies
- adult:pupil ratio
- visit preparations
- the purpose
- follow-up work

- moral issues regarding keeping animals in zoos.

The zoo visit is not what it was. You have to be prepared to defend everything you sanction in your school. It is very rare that you can in fact justify "a fun day out". That does not mean, however, that you and your school can no longer have fun! A well-planned contextual zoo visit can be enjoyable as well as informative. It is wise, however, to cover the moral issues of keeping animals in zoos. Children's thinking needs to be challenged. The content of any follow-up work will be of greater depth and more stimulating if these concerns are addressed. As in all good teaching, both sides of the argument must be presented in order to allow your pupils to form their own opinions.

Do enjoy the zoo, but watch out for lions!

BIBLIOGRAPHY and FURTHER READING

Ball, S.J. (1990) *The Micro-Politics of the School*, London and New York: Routledge.

Bruner, J.S. (1985) "Vygotsky: a historical and conceptual pespective", in Wertsch (ed.) *Culture, Communication and Cognition*, Cambridge: Cambridge University Press.

Bush, T. (ed.) (1989) *Management in Education Series*, Milton Keynes: Open University.

Children and Young Person's Act, 1989: HMSO

Craig, I. (ed.) (1989) *Primary Headship in the 1990s*, Longman, in association with The National Association of Head Teachers.

Department of Education and Science (1988) *School Governors: A Guide to the Law*, London: Central Office of Information, HMSO.

Drucker, P.F. (1989) 'The Spirit of Performance' *Management in Education Series*, Milton Keynes: Open University Press.

Duigan, P.A. (1989) "Reflective management: the key to quality leadership", in Colin Riches and Colin Morgan (eds) *Human Resource Management in Education*, Milton Keynes: Open University Press.

Fullan, M. and Hargreaves, A. (1992) *What's Worth Fighting for in Your School*, Buckingham: Open University Press.

Fullan, M. (1992) *What's Worth Fighting for in Headship*, Milton Keynes: Open University Press.

Hoyle, E. (1989) *The Micropolitics of Schools*, Milton Keynes: Open University Press.

Kyriacou, C. (1991) *Essential Teaching Skills*, Hemel Hempstead: Simon & Schuster Education.

Maclure, S. (1988) *Education Re-formed: A Guide to the Education Reform Act 1988*, Sevenoaks: Hodder & Stoughton.

Morgan, G. (1986) *Images of Organisation*, SAGE Publications.

Prendergast, S. (1992) *This Is Time to Grow Up: Girls' Experiences of Menstruation at School*, Cambridge: Health Promotion Trust.

Sallis, J. (1988) *Schools, Parents and Governors: A New Approach to Accountability*, London: Routledge.

Schiller, C. (1979) *Christian Schiller in His Own Words*, London: A. & C. Black Ltd.

Yule, W. and Gold, A. (1933) *Wise Before the Event*, Calouste Gulbenkian Foundation.